**Bearcat Wings
Maybe Too Much of a Good Thing:**

It is fascinating what the mind remembers and what it doesn't. I can't remember what I had for breakfast yesterday, but some test flights stick in my mind like they happened this afternoon. The program in which I was paid to intentionally break large parts of wings off a Grumman Bearcat while in the air and then land minus more than 20% of the wing area and half the ailerons is one of those events. I remember every aspect of that program in infinite detail. A few folks have marveled that I have such a retentive memory. But, such events became indelibly etched in the mind's eye of a 24 year old bachelor who got paid for flying experimental fighters and had yet to find out that girls existed.

The concept of intentionally shedding large portions of an aircraft's wing in flight would appear to be pure insanity until the nature of the times is examined when the Grumman F8F-1 Bearcat was in its gestation period.

A Trip to England Designs the F8F-1 Bearcat:

In late 1942 it had become clear that the Grumman Hellcat was a great improvement in fighting performance compared to the vaunted Zero fighter.

But newer enemy aircraft were on the horizon which would have much greater horsepower and performance. All students of aerial warfare knew that the fighting life of any aircraft in wartime, even the new Hellcat, would be limited.

At that same time the Pratt and Whitney engine manufacturing company had gone into mass production of the 2,000 hp R-2800-B. Thus newer engines of vastly increased horsepower were not yet available for American airplane designers. It was clear that to get further increases in performance over the Hellcat's, Grumman designers would have to produce a much smaller and lighter fighter, utilizing the R-2800-B engines which were currently in production. They could then count on planned engine performance developments later in the R-2800 development cycle.

In September 1943, three Grumman officials went to England to discuss and fly captured fighters of the Axis Powers. The team included Leroy Grumman, President of Grumman (a Navy test pilot during and after World War One), Bud Gillies, Vice President of Flight Operations (a test pilot current in all American fighters at that time), and Bob Hall, Chief of Experimental Engineering (a famous designer and

Above, XF8F-1 BuNo 90460 first flew on 31 August 1944 with Bob Hall at the controls. A small dorsal strip was added to the aft fuselage in an attempt to counteract the destabilization effects of the bubble canopy. It did not work so a full-fledged dorsal fin was installed. (Grumman)

test pilot of Gee Bee racing aircraft as well as Grumman fighters). Having been a Grumman engineering test pilot for only 6 months, I was sadly much too junior to be invited for that most fateful trip.

Of the several airplanes they saw and test flew, they were most fascinated with the new German fighter, the Focke Wulf FW-190A. It not only had sprightly performance, but excellent flight characteristics, with a weight of only 8,750 pounds combined with 1730 horsepower. This gave the FW-190A-4 a power loading of 5.02 pounds of aircraft weight per horsepower. The larger Hellcat, 3,200 pounds heavier with only 270 horsepower more than the 190 gave it a higher power loading of 6.04 pounds of aircraft weight per horsepower. Both Gillies and Hall evaluated the Focke Wulf in flight and immediately found many qualities which had to be incorporated in any new U.S.Navy fighter. The FW-190 was exactly what

1

Above, Fw190A-4 similar to the one tested in England by Leroy Grumman, Bud Giles and Bob Hall was about a foot longer and had a foot shorter wingspan than the production F8F-1 (see comparison top view below). The F8F incorporated larger tail surfaces and had slightly more wing area. (USAF via Corwin Meyer)

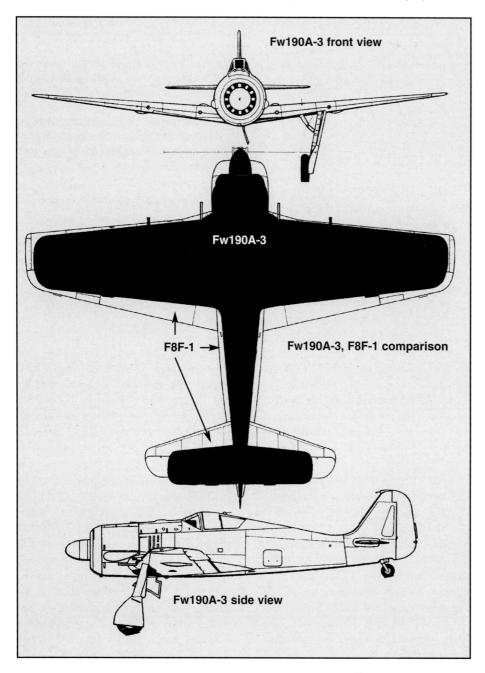

Fw190A-3 front view

Fw190A-3

F8F-1 → Fw190A-3, F8F-1 comparison

Fw190A-3 side view

the Hellcat follow-on aircraft should be. But, the Grumman team selected a more competitive power loading of 4.5 pounds of aircraft weight per horsepower as a goal.

The only two U.S.Navy requirements that it lacked were: sufficient vision angle over the nose for both good lead-computing gunnery and proper carrier approach visibility. It also needed an aero-structure that would withstand the rigors of carrier operations.

The 1942 Focke Wulf-190A had a BMW 801D-2 engine with the MW-50 water/methanol injection system to boost the engine to 2100 HP for short periods. The BMW engine also had two innovations that totally amazed them. It had an automatic, altitude-controlled, variable speed, hydramatic shifting supercharger blower with an automatic engine/throttle control that did not need pilot attention to continually obtain the maximum combat power as the aircraft's altitude changed. In essence the throttle could be left in the full forward position and full engine power would be automaticaly provided for any altitude changes during combat! This was a big advantage for the combat pilot. It allowed him to concentrate completely on the enemy and NOT the cockpit. The mechanically geared blowers of American engines required a great deal of pilot attention during combat to have maximum power available at all times. This same hydramatic labor saving shifting of gears in American aircraft engines had to wait until after the war to be produced. The second item which also reduced in-cockpit attention was a large cooling fan mounted in front of the engine which was driven by the propeller to obtain adequate engine cooling air under all ground and flight conditions.

In the same light of fighter cockpit combat improvements, the FW-190A had the first 360° clear view canopy that the team had ever seen. It was also to be a strong point of interest to the team for their next fighter.

So many aspects of the 190 impressed them that they felt compelled to hurry home and construct a fighter of this performance/weight class that would utilize the almost-ready development model of the Pratt and Whitney R-2800-C engine with 2400 War Emergency (water injection) horsepower. This would provide our Naval aviators a big performance increase over the newer 2000 HP Japanese fighters soon to appear and still retain the excellent performance and reliability of the P&W R-2800-B model series production engines presently operating in thousands of fleet Hellcats.

The Design of the American Focke Wulf:

Design of the XF8F-1 was started immediately on their return to the United States and Mr. Grumman took a direct hand in its design. As the effort progressed, it became obvious that carrier aircraft catapulting and arresting loads, not required in the Focke Wulf 190, were going to make the gross weight goal of 8750 pounds difficult to obtain in the new F8F-1 Bearcat.

Innovative measures were needed to meet the stringent weight and fuselage space goals that Mr Grumman and his team were striving for. Many items that were considered standard Navy equipment were going to have to be sacrificed. The Hellcat's standard six guns were reduced to four. The internal fuel capacity was lowered from 250 to 169 gallons. The adjustable seat with its weighty fuselage overturn structure had to be eliminated. (A simple overturn structure was required by the Navy, however, after the number two production Bearcat F8F-1 [BuNo 90428] completed its initial carrier trials aboard the USS Charger [CVE-30] in February 1945). The seat would be fixed to the cockpit floor structure. Cushions or a seat or backpack parachute would be used in place of seat adjustment for pilot size differences. The folding wing mechanism would have to be much simpler than that of the Hellcat and be moved further outboard on the wing to save weight. Instead of a three fuel tank system of the Hellcat, a single tank would sim-

plify the system and reduce the weight, too. Even with the weight and complexity reduction of the Hellcat's two stage, three-speed engine supercharger for a two-speed supercharged Bearcat engine, the bogey of 8750 pounds still seemed far from being attainable.

The First Major Hurdle Uniquely Solved:

Finally, Grumman's Chief of Structures, Pete Ehrlensen, came up with a far-out, but intriguing, idea to save a further 230 pounds of wing structure, which was a large enough chunk of weight needed to meet the goal.

Pete remembered that during my structural demonstrations in the Hellcat I had four failures at the mid-point of the stabilizers when I pulled up into the unknown compressibility "Buffet Boundry" to attain the needed 7.5Gs to meet Navy requirements. No other Grumman fighter had previously experienced this disasterous phe-

Above, 1/4 scale high speed dive flight test model of the Bearcat attached to the belly of a Navy PB-1V on 7-27-47. (USN) Bottom, XF8F-1 BuNo 90460 in the Langley Field full-scale wind tunnel testing the dorsal fin fix that was needed after "Corky" performed the first spin tests on the Bearcat. By the time of the these wind tunnel tests, the fix had already been incorporated into production aircraft for several months. (via Corwin Meyer)

nomena. We later found out that the Lockheed P-38 and the Republic P-47 had experienced this buffet boundary. The P-38 had lost complete tail sections killing two pilots while trying to meet their demonstration G points. During subsequent operational combat flying, Hellcat pilots had bent and even broken off stabilizers and elevators at mid-span too, when they entered the mysterious and unknown violent buffet boundry during high G pullouts while fighting Japanese Zeros above 10,000 feet.

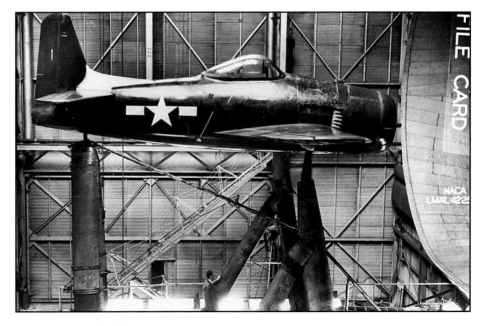

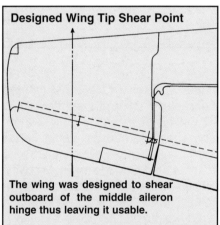

Designed Wing Tip Shear Point

The wing was designed to shear outboard of the middle aileron hinge thus leaving it usable.

Above and below, F8F-1 BuNo 95802 after an attempt to blow both wing tips off in December 1946 using only 12 inches of primer cord. Only the right wing tip seperated the aircraft, but the Bearcat's flight characteristics were hardly affected. (Grumman via Corwin Meyer)

The stabilizers and elevators fortunately broke just outboard of the mid-span hinge. In breaking, they unloaded themselves of their stress. The structural failures fortunately left enough of the tail feathers to fly the airplane back to the carrier and make a successful landing. The remaining portion of the stabilizers were much stronger because their span loading was reduced as the tail loads were now on a much shorter moment arm.

Pete thought that if the wing was designed to have an ultimate breaking load of 9 G at a controlled point about three feet inboard of the wingtip, the wing would relieve itself of the tip loads. The remainder of the wing structure would then support a load of 13Gs, the standard ultimate load of fighters at that time. The amount of wing area remaining was calculated to be sufficient to make a safe, albeit somewhat faster, carrier landing.

He suggested that a carefully designed rivet joint be made at about half span of the outer folding wing panels and a break joint be designed in the ailerons so that the outer half would also detach when the wing panels broke off. This would leave half the aileron connected by two of the three hinges to the remaining wing structure and provide lateral control for carrier landings.

It took some persuasion for the Navy to agree to such novel measures. However, wartime pressures dictated more and more climb performance requiring greater power-to-weight ratios. Grumman designers had such an outstanding reputation with the Navy Brass and pilots with experience in "Grumman Ironworks" airplanes that they finally agreed to this suggestion.

The Grumman Bearcat Finally Takes Shape:

The Grumman Bearcat design team's great enthusiasm for the FW-190 radiated throughout the small Grumman preliminary design department headed up by Dick Hutton, a long-time Grumman engineer. Because the Pratt and Whitney R-2800-C engine development program would not be completed in time, a R-

2800-B model Hellcat engine was to be installed in the first XF8F-1 prototype, Buno 90460. This was consistant with Mr. Grumman's conservative philosophy that a new aircraft must not have a new engine installed. The -C engine was programmed to be installed in the second XF8F-1 prototype, Buno 90460, which was scheduled to fly four months after the first prototype. The hydramatic variable speed drive supercharger R-2800-E engine with an FW-190-type automatic engine control (which Grumman had talked the Navy Bureau of Aeronautics and Pratt and Whitney exectuives into designing) would be installed in production aircraft only after it had been proven in its required 100 hour full power tests. Because of the many problems found in developing the -E model engine, it would not be delivered to squadrons until November 1947.

The Bearcat's All-Too-Short Ground Tests:

A very detailed ground test program was conducted to prove that the riveted connection at the break joint safey tip would sever consistantly at 9G as promised. One must realize that wing loads on every new fighter were estimated by engineering. Before the Navy approved of the contract at the inception of the program, they required that Grumman make an experimental installation of this wing-span-shortening concept on a Grumman F4F Wildcat. Grumman had to prove the outboard break joint of the wing and aileron simultaneously in a 6G flight test to demonstrate that the Wildcat had acceptable flight characteristics to make a satisfactory carrier-type landing and that Grumman engineers had predicted accurate flight loads. After successful wing tip ground tests had been demonstrated, a Grumman F4F Wildcat (BuNo 04085) was then rigged-up with the special wing safety-tip rivet joint and aileron severance capability. Grumman test pilot Carl Alber demonstrated this unique theory at 7000 feet in one flight on March 14, 1944. Both three-foot wing sections and aileron halves came off within one-tenth of a second of each

other. Everything worked as predicted. The airplane had also demonstrated more than sufficient maneuverability for a satisfactory carrier landing at only eight mph faster than the normal Wildcat approach speed. The Navy and Grumman were now satisfied that the F8F would be operationally acceptable with such an installation.

The Bearcat Flys:

The first experimental F8F-1 flew with Bob Hall at the controls on 31 August 1944, just eleven months after the Grumman team had returned from England. I was his chase pilot in an F7F-3N Tigercat, and although his

Above, XF8F-1 BuNo 90460 runs-up prior to its first flight on 31 August 1944. (Grumman) Below, Grumman test pilots Robert L. (Bob) Hall (left) and Seldon "Connie" Converse discussing a flight test of an F6F Hellcat in 1943. Bob Hall flew the Bearcat's first flight in XF8F-1 BuNo 90460 and many others. (Grumman)

25 minute flight was not very long, it was certainly mind-boggling to his chase pilot. His first comment after he landed was that the stabilizer span must be increased by two feet. Work started immediately after it was pulled into the experimental hangar. I finally

had the timerity to ask him what data he had recorded to come to such an amazing conclusion on the very first flight. He stated very calmly in his Boston accent, "I took no data. If an aircraft is completely unstable that is the only fix that will do". I was learning from a pro.

On 8 September 1944, after his fourth flight, he turned it over to me to open the flight flutter envelope speed in order to determine the Bearcat's maximum level flight performance at all altitudes.

My first flight in the Bearcat was probably the most exciting I have ever experienced in my flying career. The takeoff was exhilirating beyond my wildest dreams and required more talent than my Hellcat-trained capabilities. With flaps extended one third deflection (15°) the Bearcat would take-off in less than half the Hellcat's distance and several times before I had been able to advance the throttle to full power! I immediately found that I had to climb steeply in order to be able to retract the landing gear before exceeding the landing gear down maximum speed. Of course, this very

steep and showy climb-out attitude became satisfying to me knowing how much I was entertaining the onlookers. On my first full-power climb to the F8F-1's service ceiling of 40,650 feet, we found that the Bearcat with the Hellcat's -B model engine had over twice the Hellcat's 3200 feet-per-minute rate-of-climb!

Flutter flight testing was then performed by increasing the aircraft's speed 25 mph at a time in level flight and making stick jabs with the my fist, both longitudinally, laterally and rudder foot jabs, to see if there were any latent flutter tendencies in the three flight control systems. This procedure was continued until the maximum level flight speed was attained from 30,000 feet to sea level at 5000 foot intervals. It was the same simple historic method flutter test used since the Wright Brothers era. Fortunately for me, Grumman's flight control balancing philosophy (to guarantee no flutter) required 100% static balance in the elevator and aileron and rudder control. Because of the high weight of the lead mass balances required for 100% static balance, many other fighter company designers believed

that 50% mass balance in all three controls was sufficient. They experienced destructive wing and horizontal tail flutter too many times, and many test pilots were lost during the 1930s and 40s. I am still here because Mr. Grumman had been a very conservative and knowledgable test pilot even after he quit flying fighters after the end of WW-II at the age of 50!

After these flights were completed, the XF8F-1 had demonstrated a top speed of 455 mph which pleased both Grumman and the Navy.

The High Speed Dives Commence:

Before getting into this phase of the structural testing, I would like to explain the unique instrumentation that the Bearcat was forced into because of its small fuselage internal volume and critical aft CG condition.

Below, "Corky" Meyers at the controls took over Bearcat testing on the aircraft's (BuNo 90460) fifth flight on 8 September 1944. (Grumman via Corkey Meyer)

The normal instrumentation of the test Hellcat consisted of a very large, heavy photopanel which duplicated all of the many cockpit instruments, plus a recording movie camera and a large 36 channel oscillograph for structural measurements, all installed in the spacious aft fuselage. In the test Bearcat instrumentation, the recording camera was simply installed under my left arm, pointing to the six most vital flight instruments in the cockpit. The strucural oscillograph recording equipment was reduced from 36 to 12 channels and attached to the pilot's armor plate in its much smaller aft fuselage compartment. A 50 pound weight was added to the propeller hub to complete the balance of the aircraft at its most forward CG. With the camera under my left elbow, the Bearcat's cockpit became slightly more cramped for its six-foot-two pilot.

With the level flight performance program completed, the original preflight pullout limit of 5Gs would now be upped to 7.5G in preparation for attaining the limit dive indicated speed of 540 mph. This was 40 mph above the Hellcat limit speed. I realized that I would have to be very careful in creeping up to this speed in order to avoid transonic compressibility "frozen controls" problems I had encountered in the Hellcat's final demonstration.

The demonstration was begun in the first production Bearcat, BuNo 90437, on 5 February 1945. After the airspeed and instrumentation calibrations were completed, pullouts were begun at 30,000 feet to determine the buffet boundry limit that occurred when wing lift could no longer increase the Gs by pulling further aft on the stick. These pullouts were performed at 5000 foot increments to sea level over the full speed range of the Bearcat. In this manner, we determined that the Navy requirement of 7.5G at 7,500 feet could be met at any altitude below 13,000 feet. The two final Navy demonstration points of 7.5G were able to be demonstrated easily at 7,500 feet altitude at 350 mph and 460 mph. The Navy final dive limit requirement was only 3.5G

at 540 mph because of now expected compressibility effects. As the dive speeds increased above level flight speeds the stick and rudder jabs were inserted before the pullouts to complete the flutter program. All of the dives with 7.5G pullouts were accomplished to the Navy's satisfaction.

The Final Max Speed Dive Was Much More Difficult:

From my previous dives I determined that I would need to start this final dive from 25,000 feet at no more than a 45° dive angle to keep from entering the unknown and the scary transonic compressibility region. I was successful in keeping out of the compressibility area, but just as I completed my flutter jabs and before I started my 3.5G pullout a loud explosion occurred, filling the cockpit with mist. The aircraft instantly pitched up to 8.5G without any action of mine! I jammed the stick forward with all my might and yanked the throttle back to

Above, the first production F8F-1 BuNo 90437 with test stainless steel trough cowling around the engine's exhaust which was fitted while exploring the unexplained spanwise flow on the wing during the maximum speed dive tests. The fix, which also included the combining of the five exhaust pipes into three, which raised the exhaust exit four more inches above the wing, worked. The structure behind the pilot's headrest was a movie camera that took film of the upper surface of the tufted wing to check the reduction of spanwise flow. The blunt spinner on the propeller was a 25lb steel weight used to attain full forward cg for these flights. (Grumman via Corwin Meyer) Below, the fifth production F8F-1 BuNo 90441 was temporarilly used for the structural demonstration after the unexpected extension of the port landing gear on BuNo 90437. This aircraft still had the original five exhaust pipe system. This is the aircraft that had a faulty port landing gear microswitch indicator which caused it to collapse on me even with a "full-down" cockpit indication. (Grumman via Corwin Meyer)

the idle stop.

When I came to my senses at about 200 mph and 5000 feet higher, my chase pilot Carl Alber calmly suggested that I really didn't need to extend my left landing gear because we were not at pattern altitude for the Grumman airport. He then seriously reported that my left landing gear had extended at the maximum speed and the ballast-filled ammunition boxes had disappeared through the bottom of the wing. He added that a small amount of smoke was coming from the open left landing gear wheel well. He continued to inspect the aircraft after I extended the right gear and tail wheel to see if they were available for landing. The landing was anti-climactic, but the flight was not over by a long sight.

I tried to crank the canopy open for landing but it wouldn't budge no matter how hard I tried to pull the crank with both hands. Later inspection showed that the aft end of the canopy had jumped its rails and was several inches to the left of its normal position. Because my plane captain didn't want to damage the canopy with any improper actions, it took twenty long minutes for him to finally free and remove the canopy for my belated exit. It was soon determined that the excessive air loads on the canopy caused by the large angle yaw to the left, which had ocurred when the left landing gear extended, caused the aft end of the canopy to jump its rails by three inches. It was also determined that the smoke came from the engine's oil cooler. The excessive 8.5G had broken the oil cooler mounting straps and cracked one line fitting causing oil to leak onto the exhaust stacks.

The undesired extension of the left landing gear was caused by the up-lock hook, which grasped the landing gear latch, not having sufficient strength and bending under high speed air loads. Pull forces imposed during subsequent ground tests demonstrated that it could be too easily bent and therefore unlatched. The hook was redesigned and proof tested to estimated structural and air

Above and below, F8F-1 BuNo 90438 flown by NATC pilots for carrier suitability tests on the USS Charger (CVE-30) in February 1945. With a 25 mph wind over the deck, it took only 225 ft for the Bearcat to take off during a free deck launch. This was only 60% of the distance required by the Hellcat. (USN)

loads of 9G on an F8F-1 landing gear in a test rig. All the Bearcats were grounded and retrofitted with the stronger up-lock hooks. We soon found out that we were not out of the woods with landing gear problems yet.

The Second F8F-1 is Instrumented For the Max Speed Dive:

Because of the excessive wing loads imposed on the first demonstration Bearcat during that 8.5G pullout, it was determined to select the fifth production F8F-1 (BuNo 90441) and instrument it to repeat the 540 mph speed dive and 3.5G pullout demonstration.

During the normal extension of the landing gear on the third build-up flight, I had a left landing gear "barber pole" indication which meant the gear was not locked down. I then performed all of the required bounces on the runway in both right and left yawed skidding conditions with many runway observers to get a locked indication of the left landing gear, which it did. The runway observers agreed that the left landing gear seemed locked down and radioed their decision to me. I shouldn't have listened!

I landed uneventfully until I made the left turn into the parking area. The left gear collapsed inboard with a crash before I had made half the required turn. It is amazing how fast a propeller comes to a stop under those conditions. Of course, I immediately realized that I should have rolled to a stop on the runway without turning so that my plane captain could make a visual check of the down locks. And, my incident happened directly in front of the Plant Five "mahogany row" for all management to see. Engineering and inspection determined that the Bearcat's down lock indicator microswitch had been set at the end of its operational range, instead of in the middle of the range (to make up for any structural deflections occurring from flight loads), and therefore it had not been properly positioned with the completed down-lock actuation. This was rectified by a manufacturing change order for all F8F-1 micro

switch adjustment procedures.

Engineering also determined that the imposed loads, which had broken the folding safety tip, and the loads at the wing root as the wing hit the ground, eliminated this aircraft from performing any further Navy demonstrations. It was tested and inspected after installing a completely new left wing, given a ground proof test to 7.5Gs, and delivered to the Navy five weeks later.

Above, the dive recovery flaps in their 20° open position. These small flaps have always seemed fantastic to me in that they had the power to change a stick-frozen, unrecoverable diving Bearcat into a recovered, docile fighter in about five seconds. They licked compressibility problems until fighter wings became much thinner. Transonic problems then disappeared. (Grumman via Corwin Meyer) Below, the dive recovery flaps in their retracted position. They were located under the wing just aft of the landing gear wells. (Grumman via Corwin Meyer)

Above, XF8F-1 BuNo 90460 assigned to NACA on 5 February 1945 for wind tunnel tests. (NACA) Below, F8F-1 BuNo 90448 in one of NACA's wind tunnels was operated at Langley from 4 January through 18 February 1946. A second F8F-1, BuNo 94812, was operated from 21 May 1946 through 17 April 1947. A third F8F-1, BuNo 94873, was operated from 6 June 1946 through most of 1951. (NACA)

The First Bearcat Re-Appears:

Happily, inspection and engineering had since cleared the first instrumented demonstration Bearcat (BuNo 90437) for flight after performing a full set of ground proof tests and approved it for flight. Therefore, it was decided to use that aircraft to complete the Navy demonstration. The repeat of the max speed dive was anticlimatic without any further

destruction of my ego.

In March of 1945, the Navy decided to equip all Bearcats with the NACA dive recovery flaps so that easy recoveries could be performed after the transonic compressibility regime had been entered. A full power, terminal velocity vertical dive was required to be demonstrated from the service ceiling with an acceptable 4G recovery.

I completed three full power dives beyond the Bearcat's critical .76 Mach number limit on 7 April 1945, finally increasing the dive angle to the vertical. I attained .785, .805 and .815 Mach number with 4G pullouts using the dive recovery flaps at about 29,000 feet after denser air had begun to reduce the Mach number as the altitude decreased. The Bearcat exhibited the same impossible recovery, stick freezing and nose down dive characteristics that the Hellcat

and Tigercat had shown in their compressibility dives. The dive recovery flaps worked perfectly. The Bearcat structural demonstration was finally completed.

The Bearcat Demonstrates the First Navy Rolling Pullout:

The Bearcat was required to perform a completely new maneuver that the Navy had just added to their repertoire of F8F-1 structural requirements: the rolling pullout. This maneuver required the pilot to slam the stick over to full deflection at the required air speed/altitude combination in less than one tenth of a second and pull 5 Gs after the aircraft had attained its maximum rolling velocity. It was decided to practice these dives in a Grumman F4F-4 Wildcat (BuNo 4085) which had a fantastic history of combat structural integrity. The Wildcat had an 11 inch lateral stick throw from neutral position and I soon found out that getting the stick over to the full left deflection in one-tenth of a second took a lot of shoulder and back twisting while keeping the shoulder harness properly tightened. Performing rolling pullout maneuvers in the Bearcat, with its six-and-a-half inch full lateral stick deflection, was much easier. I performed twelve build-up maneuvers both right and left at three increasing air speeds until 5G was demonstrated in dives at 425 mph at 7500 feet. I was pleased that this portion of the structural demonstration was completed.

I ferried this Bearcat to the Naval Air Test Center (NATC), Patuxent River, MD, and performed the complete structural and flight maneuver demonstrations to the satisfaction of the Navy witnesses from 5 to 11 May 1945.

The Bearcat Flys With Asymmetric Wings:

As part of the F8F-1 Bearcat demonstration, the Navy required that Grumman make takeoffs and landings with one right and one left wing tip and aileron panel removed to demonstrate acceptable flight characteristics for landing safely aboard a

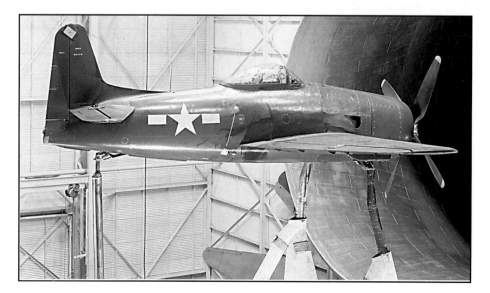

carrier in case only one tip came off during a high G air maneuver.

I flew those tests with the second XF8F-1 (BuNo 90461) on 5 and 6 April 1945. Although there were minor unsymmetrical lateral and directional flight deficiencies, it was determined that the airplane had acceptable flight characteristics if only a maximum of 15° of landing flap were used. Carrier approach speeds were increased by 10 mph. If more than 15° of flaps were used, the airplane reacted with much too strong wing heaviness on the side of the short wing during landing approach turns. WWII carriers, however, were well capable of handling the increase in landing speed requirements. Both Grumman and the Navy were satisfied with the results of these tests.

Bearcat Spins Were Most Educational:

The standard Navy spin requirement for the Bearcat was 5 turn right and left upright spins, 2 turn right and left inverted spins and one turn landing condition spins. The NACA (now NASA) Bearcat model tests in their vertical spin tunnel had clearly demonstrated normal spin entry and recovery characteristics in both upright and inverted spins.

To be sure that the XF8F-1 Bearcat (BuNo 90461) had all the safety precautions possible in case it didn't duplicate the spin tunnel results, an eight foot anti-spin parachute on a fifty foot nylon lanyard was installed to be deployable by the pilot in case unrecoverable spin tendencies appeared during the tests.

During the first ground test of the spin chute with the engine running at full power the spin chute deployed properly after my actuation from the cockpit, but it would not release from the aircraft when I pulled the deployment control. It remained solidly attached, swinging back and forth in the slipstream instead of releasing.

Inspection after the test showed that one of the jaws of the release mechanism, which were perfect cir-

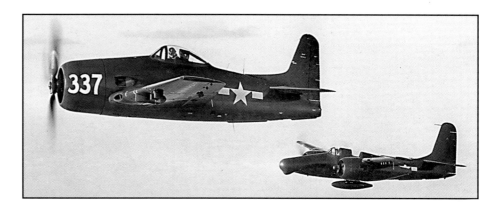

cles, had ground into the metal ring of the chute lanyard attachment sufficiently to prevent its sliding off of the open jaw. If the deployed chute wouldn't have released in the air the chute's high drag would have made the aircraft totally unflyable, even with full power.

With engineering's approval, I filed the open ends of the hook jaw ends a few degrees for relief. In the many following ground pull tests after chute deployment, it now released every time from the aircraft after the jaws opened. Subsequent air tests also demonstrated satisfactory anti-spin chute drag and release so spins were set for the next day, 19 February 1945. It now appeared that spinning the Bearcat would be a simple task. It wasn't!

The historic proper safe spin procedure in new aircraft is to perform

Above, F8F-1 BuNo 95337 piloted by Pat Gallo flying chase for F7F-3N BuNo 80330 during its external stores research program in 1946, piloted by "Corky" Meyer. (Grumman via Corwin Meyer) Below, the white lines at the leading edge of the landing flaps was a flap gap seal that was installed on an early Bearcat to get less drag and thus more level flight speed. It worked so well that all the Bearcats had it installed in production. (Grumman via Corwin Meyer)

spin entries and recoveries increasing a half-turn at a time until after two or three turns have definitely shown the pilot that the spin had stabilized in both rate of turn and a nose down attitude well below the horizon. The first half turn, full turn and one-and-a-half turn spin attempts showed normal recoveries in less than a turn. In the following two-turn spin, the nose rose

most amazed to find myself hanging straight down viewing the icy waters of Long Island Sound rushing up at me. I rapidly actuated the release mechanism and recovered from the vertical dive. The chute released and floated gently into the Sound. I then returned to Grumman now a much more highly educated test pilot in believing NACA model spin tunnel results and anti-spin chute capabilities.

The Bearcat Gets A More Powerful Tail.

From the vast experience of Bob Hall's spin testing background he decided that the Bearcat needed more directional stability at the high angle of attack of spins. This is because the vertical fin and rudder operate in the very low-energy wing stall wake air in upright spins. Therefore a three-inch deep, seven feet long, ventral fin was added to the bottom of the fuselage and a large dorsal fin was installed in front of the Bearcat's normal fin. Flight tests showed that the Bearcat's directional stability at full rudder pedal, maximum yaw angles at stall/spin airspeeds had increased substantially.

Above, test pilot Pat Gallo posing just before performing a Grumman open house airshow in F8F-1 Bearcat BuNo 90455 during the summer of 1946. Below, F8F Bearcat (left) and F6F Hellcat (right) make a high speed pass over a small airshow crowd in 1945. (Ginter collection)

rapidly to the horizon after one-and-a-half turns telling me that a flat, unre-

coverable spin had started. I applied full anti-spin rudder and elevator control deflections with absolutely no signs of aircraft recovery. After waiting a turn to see if the aircraft would finally react to the controls, I decided that the anti-spin chute deployment was now mandatory. It deployed instantly, yanked the aircraft out of its spin rotation and dropped the Bearcat's nose to the vertical. I was

All of the next upright spins progressed satisfactorily showing stabilized spin rates and nose down attitudes through the five-turn spins requiring only one-turn recovery after anti-spin controls were applied. Inverted spins have the fin and rudder in the higher energy air stream; therefore the two-turn inverted spins were performed with less than one turn required for recovery without a problem.

On 27 April 1945, I flew the spin Bearcat to the Naval Air Test Center at Patuxent River, Maryland, and completed the official F8F-1 spin demonstration satisfactorily to Navy witnesses.

The F8F-2 Spins Fatally Injure Pat Gallo:

Whenever an experimental aircraft has a major change, like the new 2300 hp R-2800E-30W engine instal-

lation in the XF8F-2 Bearcat, the Navy requires rechecks of maximum structural limit dive speeds and spins. In August 1947, Grumman test pilot Pat Gallo had completed the dive tests on the XF8F-2 (BuNo 95330) prototype and was preparing to start spin tests.

The aircraft had a similar anti-spin chute release mechanism to the one that I had used in the XF8F-1 spins, but it had not been reworked to provide the jaw relief angle change that I had needed to guarantee its release in the air. On his flight to check its deployment and release from the aircraft, it had the same hang-up that I had found on ground tests and did not release from the aircraft. The aircraft became uncontrollable and Pat bailed out, but he was to a low to the ground for his personal parachute to open and was fatally injured. The jaws were reworked and the anti-spin chute deployment and release tests and aircraft spin tests were completed satisfactorily.

Flight Proof of the Bearcat's Wingtip Weight Saving Device:

A very detailed design and ground test program was conducted of the shedable three-foot safety wingtip and aileron half by Grumman engineering on XF8F-1 (BuNo 90460) before it made its first flight.

The Navy also specified in the Bearcat contract that an early F8F-1 aircraft demonstrate a two-flight program of a take-off and landing on each flight with a wing tip panel and half an aileron removed. One flight with the left side removed and the other with just the right ones removed. The flights were meant to demonstrate that the handling in air manuevers and carrier landing characteristics were acceptable in case only one wing tip section failed during a flight.

I had the duty to perform these two flights on the second experimental XF8F-1 Bearcat (BuNo 90461) on 4-5 April 1945. I found that general flight characteristics with one wing half three feet shorter than the other

were not as unacceptably dissimilar to the complete wing Bearcat as I had expected. Aileron and rudder trim tabs could easily handle gust turbulence or maneuvering conditions required when cruising back to the carrier, and that if only the fifteen degree landing flap selection were selected, the normal approach speed only needed to be increased 10 mph to make a satisfactory carrier approach and landing. Tests with 30° and 45° landing flap settings caused too much rolloff towards the short wing during gusts and carrier approach maneuvering.

In hindsight, it would be easy to reflect that such a meager ground and flight testing program would be grossly insufficient for such a unique innovation. The reader must remember, however, that it was wartime with the invasion of Japan imminent. Therefore, high aircraft production rates were paramount. For instance, during a single month, March 1944, when the Bearcat was in its very early design phase, Grumman delivered 620 Hellcats and 85 other aircraft including F7F Tigercats and many amphibians, which set a record for

Above, first production F8F-1 BuNo 90437 in early 1945 during the structural demonstrations. The black and white stripes on the elevators were used for determining fabric distortions during high Mach number dives. The barely visible tufts on the white center-section of the wing were photographed by two cameras in the fuselage to visualize the unwanted spanwise airflow during high Mach number pullups. (Grumman via Corwin Meyer) Below, unflattering aft-end view of XF8F-1 BuNo 90460. (Grumman)

aircraft production that stood until the end of the war. In the rush of the times, it seemed to Grumman and the Navy that the testing program was indeed sufficient. As you will see, we and the Navy underestimated the quality and quantity of our design and testing phase by an order of magnitude in order to get Bearcats in squadron quantities to the Pacific theatre ASAP!

Navy Evaluations of the Bearcat:

The First experimental XF8F-1 Bearcat was flown to the Joint

appears to have it will be rated as the top interceptor...Excellent if firepower is sufficient...This is a first class fighter which has very high maneuverability and a well-knit feeling...I rate it easily tops in Navy fighters from a combat point of view."

After I completed the spin and air maneuvers demonstration at NATC Patuxent River, MD, on 4-5 April 1945 in the second XF8F-1. I left that aircraft at Patuxent. We had completed our use of it as Bearcats were now coming off the production line. CDR Tom Connelly (who was later to become Deputy Commander of Naval Operations for Air during the F-14 Tomcat program) made an evaluation and gave me a complete rundown on his comments made during his flight. He was most enthusiastic about every aspect of our new Bearcat and required me to take specific notes of his likes and very few dislikes for me to take back to Grumman for fixes. I remember that his dislikes were only four switch locations in the cockpit. They were immediately relocated in all production aircraft upon my return to Grumman.

The Navy Final Approval of the Bearcat:

The Navy Bureau of Inspection and Survey Report gave high praise to the Bearcat, which completed those tests without encountering any major difficulties. Not only was it an exciting airplane to fly, it was 81mph faster than the Hellcat. In a 25 mph wind over the carrier deck, it took off in 200 feet compared to the Hellcat's 325 feet. It had an amazing rate-of-climb of 6,340 feet-per-minute, which was more than twice the Hellcat's and the fastest rate-of-climb of any pro-

Above, VF-19, the Navy's first operational Bearcat squadron, was at sea headed for the war zone when the war ended. The aircraft carried a yellow capitol "K" followed by the ship number, in this case 18 on the fuselage and the tail. (USN) Below, F8F-2, F7F-3N and FJ-1 at NATC during the fighter competion in 1948. (Jim Hawkins)

Army/Navy Fighter Conference in October of 1945 to permit Navy and Marine test pilots and a few select Army Air Corps pilots to evaluate it. Specific military test pilot comments from the official JA/NFC report: "Outstanding rate of climb...If the aircraft has the performance that it

peller-driven fighter in the war. Its rate-of-climb endeared it to Navy pilots because getting on top of the enemy had been the prime criteria for aerial combat success ever since World War One. Carrier deck officers were quick to note that Bearcats were very compact aircraft and that fifty could be spotted on the deck space required for thirty-six Hellcats. You can imagine that Naval aviators also enjoyed the fact that the F8F-1 Bearcat could easily out-perform all the latest P-51, P-47 and P-38 Army Air Corps fighters that were training near Navy operational squadron bases. The Bearcat was therefore immediately rushed into the fleet.

On 21 May 1945, less than nine months after the first prototype was flown, F8F-1s were delivered to VF-19, commanded by CDR Joe Smith, at NAAS Santa Rosa, CA, where operational training was begun in preparation for deployment on the USS Langley (CVL-27) in early August 1945. VF-19 was enroute to the Western Pacific combat zone when the two atom bombs were dropped and the Japanese surrendered. Bearcats just missed combat.

Bearcat Wing Safey Tip Operational Problems:
After a few months of glowing Bearcat operational reports, the Grumman Service department reported that an operational pilot had shed one of his two wingtips during a dive-bombing pullout and had augered in. Another followed soon after. The wing tips weren't coming off as designed so Grumman hurriedly sent a team of engineers to visit the squadrons to study the remains of the aircraft to find out what had gone wrong. It became apparent that the severe vibrations that the wing outer panels received from carrier landings, and the very strong wing oscillations when the airplane pulled into the buffet boundry during simulated combat maneuvers, were putting a greater fatigue strain on the special wing tip rivet joints than was predicted. In hindsight, these strains hadn't been considered sufficiently by Grumman or the Navy in the rush of getting the Bearcat into production and service. It

was also determined that the rivet joint had not received proper quality control attention in the Grumman production line. The flight envelope was imediately restricted to 5G combat maneuvers.

Wing Tip Fix Number One:
Because of the great need for the Bearcat's superiority of performance over enemy fighters, the Navy and Grumman soon agreed on another method to guarantee wingtip separation and which did not depend solely on the specialized rivet joint that took such a beating in many flight regimes.

Above, a production F8F-2 crashed by Grumman test pilot Tommy Le-Boutillier in 1948. He had an engine failure, overshot a dead stick landing, tore off a wing going through the trees at about 30ft altitude, rolled over and went through a house inverted. A lady was ironing when the Bearcat's wing cut through the house just missing her head. The only injury was Tommy's broken little finger. (Grumman via Corwin Meyer) Below, LeBoutillier getting ready for his next flight in another F8F-2 the day after the crash. From left to right are: Grumman Test Pilot Victor Eble, Joey Gaeta, Tower Manager Lou Salvante and Chief Test Pilot Connie Converse. (Grumman)

Above, F8F-1 on 20 March 1945 with wings folded. (Grumman) Below, F8F-1 drop test ship with weight fitted in place of an engine on 29 January 1945. (Grumman)

One idea that should have solved the problem was to install a 12-inch strip of prima cord (a rope-type explosive cord used to detonate dynamite) just outboard of both wing rivet-joints on the lower wing skins, actuated by electrical micro-switches at both break joints that would fire the other tip's explosive device after the first wingtip came off. We called them "ice box" (door light) switches, which shows our technical nomenclature antiquity! The ground tests were

spectacular, to say the least. After several successful tests, we rigged a Bearcat with this Fourth-of-July system.

For a practical test the left wingtip was structured to come off at 5G and according to theory, the "ice box" microswitch in the other wing would electrically activate the prima cord to blow the other 7.5G designed tip off at the same instant.

450 mph at 7500 feet altitude in a 30° dive angle was selected for the demonstration point. We had movie photographers on both sides of my Bearcat in the rear cockpits of F7F-3N chase aircraft to record the action. I pulled 5.5G to insure that the 5G

rivet joint would fail and activate the other wingtip explosive.

With an impressive flash of fire, smoke and debris, the weakened tip left the aircraft as predicted at 5G but the other tip remained attached. My chase pilot inspected the trauma that had occurred to the wings. He observed a large hole in the bottom skin of the right wingtip, which proved that the prima cord had fired as predicted, but the wingtip remained firmly attached even though the 12x4-inch explosion hole was in the most critical wing stress area. Fortunately, the massive hole in the wing did not cause any flutter disturbance to the aileron as might be expected. As I had already landed the F8F with left tip removed, I was ready for the experience again.

Wing Tip Fix Number Two:
It was quite obvious during the debrief that there were a lot of very perplexed engineers. Finally, one engineer timidly offered the suggestion that possibly 450 mph slipstream effects had not been considered sufficiently. So, back to the old drawing board.

The project engineer suggested that a full wing chord of 26 inches of prima cord be used on the next flight after ground tests were run to check if that amount of explosion would not be too strong and cause other wing damage. On the next flight when I pulled 6G, both tips departed as planned amid much smoke and debris flying from the airplane. Even though the prima cord made a deafening explosion during ground tests, I could not hear it in the cockpit. Both chase pilots were much more excited than I was from seeing the visual effects that I couldn't see while monitoring the G accelerometer in the cockpit. They said that it looked like the airplane had blown up. There were two very smoky explosions, two wing tips and two aileron halves coming off in rapid succession, along with much shattered metal from the explosion areas. The wing tip ends were cleanly severed as hoped for with no other damage. There weren't even small metal shards remaining on the wing

or aileron ends to suggest that an explosion had done the surgery. The test was considered a great success by both the Navy and Grumman. (Incidentally, we stuffed both the departing wing sections with Kapok so we could pick them up floating in the Long Island Sound where we were performing the flight tests).

The Navy now required Grumman to do a complete flight envelope demonstration versus the one-shot, war-time demos that we had previously performed. Consequently, a program was developed that pulled the wingtips off from 200 mph to the limit dive speed of the Bearcat.

During the wingtip severance at 5G, I had noticed that the airplane had pitched up to 6.5G, one more G than I had tried to attain. Being the structural demonstration test pilot for the F4F, F6F, F7F and F8F, I had made hundreds of pullups and had been able to target within one-tenth of a G of of my requirement. So this excessive G bothered me. I talked to the engineers about it but they suggested that I was probably nervous—strongly implying pilot error as they usually did when they couldn't think up a satisfactory answer. I promptly and wrongly put this slur on my talents out of my mind.

We then beefed-up both wing tip riveted joints to the full 7.5G demo point, armed the 26-inch prima cord devices and proceeded with the complete program. On the first pullout, I aimed at 8G to be sure one or the other joints would fail. They came off with the usual fireworks, and after it was all over, I noticed that the maximum G that was recorded was 9.5! I came back and emphatically stated that I couldn't have overshot that much and demanded an explanation from the aerodynamics department using some indelicate, seldom used four-letter engineering terms. After a little re-thinking another aerodynamicist observed that the airplane would certainly pitch up an additional 1.5G without pilot effort when the span, area and aspect ratio of the wing had changed the aircraft's pitching moments so drastically. He had cal-

culated that 9.5G was exactly the amount of G that the F8F should have pitched up to. So much for pilot error when engineering couldn't explain a phenomenon.

I was exonerated, but I learned that engineers who have a proprietary interest in a program may not always think as objectively as professional test flying requires when the answer is not patently obvious. That hard experience stood by me during all of my years as an experimental test pilot when I couldn't get answers that would rationally satisfy me. I began seeking two or more professional opinions long before that was an accepted practice in difficult medical prognostications.

We finished the program without much ado and the additional pitching problems were noted in the pilot's handbook for information (now that we had an explanation acceptable to engineering!) The Navy was happy with the Bearcat for full operational utilization and all aircraft were fitted

Above and below, on 8 August 1945, LT Schertz took off in F8F-1 BuNo 94841 at 14:12 for a delivery flight to NAS Floyd Bennett Field. He returned to Grumman 18 minutes later and attempted to land. After rolling 800 feet, the aircraft stood on its nose and went over on its back sliding for a distance. This aircraft was built without an over-turn structure and the fate of the pilot is not known. (Grumman)

out with the now-proven explosive systems.

Wing Tip Fix Number Three:

But our travails were not over by a long shot. The prima cord was actuated electrically but we forgot safeguards for possible ground maintainence errors. Shortly afterward, we received word from a squadron that during maintenance there was a short circuit when making some electrical tests and the wingtips of one Bearcat blew off in the hangar deck and fatal-

Above, one Bearcat, one Tigercat and four Hellcats in outdoor final assembly at Grumman in 1945. (Grumman) Below, XF8F-1 BuNo 90460 made its first flight on 31 August 1944 and was delivered on 26 February 1945. (Grumman)

---

ly injured a Navy maintenance whitehat.

The Final Wing Tip Fix:

The Navy now said that they had had enough of this special Bearcat weight-saving solution and required that the wing tips be riveted firmly to the wing without the prima cord device. The airplane flight envelope was then lmited to 4G. What with the strains of carrier landings along with pilots easily exceeding 4G in combat maneuvers and not reporting it, the Bearcat had two accidents with a half wing breaking off in the air at the wing root. A steel strap fix was installed to give all Bearcats sufficient strength for carrier landings and 7.5G in the

air, but the F8F series aircraft were soon supplanted in operational squadrons by the Grumman Panther and the McDonnell Banshee jet fighters, with much higher combat speeds and strength than the Bearcat.

Bearcat Production History:

A contract for two thousand F8F-1s was awaded in October 1944. A few documents list the first 23 aircraft as XF8F-1s, but they were listed as production aircraft in all Grumman records. The order was increased in April 1945 to over 4000 aircraft. Although the Navy had ordered 43 jet-powered McDonnell FD-1 (later changed to FH-1) Phantom fighters in January 1943, they had many doubts about its insufficient carrier performance capability and its early Westinghouse J30 jet engine reliability.

In January 1945, the Navy made plans to change Grumman production from Hellcats to Bearcats in early 1946. The Navy subsequently decided to continue both the Hellcat and

the Bearcat production lines at Grumman. At that same, however, they also decided to supplant F4F-4 Wildcat production at the General Motors Eastern Aircraft Corporation at Linden, NJ, with the Bearcat to significantly augment Bearcat combat squadron numbers before the invasion of Japan scheduled for early 1946. A letter of intent for 1,876 Bearcats was issued in February 1945 for General Motors to build the F8F-1, designated F3M-1.

In order to give GM an example to help assist production start-up, I delivered the thirty-seventh production F8F-1 (BuNo 94765) to Linden on June 10, 1945. The General Motors F3M-1 production was cancelled in August 1945 shortly after the end of the war and long before production deliveries had begun.

Although the Grumman work force was reduced from 33,046 to just under 2300 people less than a week after V-J Day, the F8F-1 production was not reduced from the early production numbers. This order made Bearcats available in large squadron numbers for the Cold War with Russia, which had started almost immediately after the end of WWII.

The Grumman test pilot group was reduced from over 50 personnel to 8. I was retained as the Senior Engineering Test Pilot, much to my relief. Although I had completed the F8F-1 Bearcat final demonstration at NATC Patuxent River, MD, in May of 1945, I was still in the middle of a long, scheduled research program on the F7F-3N Tigercat that would continue well into 1946.

The following model variants were incorporated during the four year (1945 to 1949) squadron history of the Bearcat.

XF8F-1: The standard Navy procurement of two prototypes (Buno 90460 and 90461) was concluded in March 1944 with the first aircraft to be powered with the Pratt and Whitney R-2800-10B (Hellcat) engine and the second with the newly developed R-2800-22W (water injection) C engine.

They flew respectively on 31 August 1944 and 2 December 1944. The first was flown by Bob Hall and the second was flown by the author. BuNo 90460 was used for carrier arrested landings and catapult takeoffs by the Navy at NAS Mustin Field in Philadelphia in late November 1944. It was returned to Grumman after satisfactory operations from these tests in early January 1945. It was flown to NACA Ames, Sunnyvale, CA, and put into their full-scale tunnel for 30 days to check all of the fixes that we had already flight checked satisfactorily; after that it was delivered to NATC Patuxent River in February 1945 for armament tests. It crashed there in March 1945. The second XF8F-1 (BuNo 90461) was delivered to NATC Patuxent River, after the author completed the spin and air maneuvers satisfactorily there on 27 April 1945, for evaluation by Navy test pilots. It was surveyed at Patuxent in 1946.

F8F-1: Six hundred and sixty-four F8F-1 aircraft were delivered from January 1945 to November 1947. Four were used as two-each prototypes for the XF8F-1N and XF8F-2 and 226 for F8F-1C (20mm cannon) aircraft. They were powered with the 2100 HP Pratt and Whitney R-2800-34W engine and had their fuel capacity increased from 162 to 183 gallons.

An external rack was provided underneath the fuselage for a 150 gallon drop tank or 1000 pound bomb. Just outboard of the landing gear another rack was fitted to carry either a 100, 150 or 300 gallon fuel tank, a 1000 pound bomb, an 11.75 inch Tiny Tim rocket, or a Mk-1 twin .50 caliber gun pod. Beginning with the 201st production Bearcat (BuNo 94929), two Mk-9 racks for 5-inch HVAR rockets or 100 pound bombs were added to each wing just outboard of the main wing rack location.

Grumman trials in the first XF8F-1 had shown that the Bearcat had reduced directional stability in high dive speeds with the 150 gallon drop tank installed. Experimental fins on the drop tanks eliminated the problem but the Navy would not agree to

Above, F8F-1 BuNo 94873 at NAS Patuxent River on 23 March 1946. Note foothold and handhold on the fuselage side at either end of the thin white stripe. (National Archives) Below, VF-171 F8F-1B demonstrates a field catapult take-off on 23 October 1948. The F8F-1B had four 20mm cannons instead of the four .50 cal machine guns found on the F8F-1. (via Dave Lucabaugh)

install these unilaterally on their 150 gallon tanks just for the Bearcat. The USAF had installed stabilizing fins on all their several types of fighter drop tanks for the same reason. Therefore, Grumman proposed to the Navy that a 12-inch taller fin and rudder would be required to allieviate the drop tank problem and to decrease the strong

Above, the one-off F8F-1C BuNo 94803 during prototype testing at Patuxent River, MD, on 28 September 1945. Subsequent aircraft were designated F8F-1Bs. (USN) Below, drone control prototype F8F-1D BuNo 90456 was converted in 1949. Drone control aircraft had engine blue-grey fuselages, yellow tails and wings, and red-orange wing stripes and rudder. (USN)

torque effect during take-off and carrier wave-off maneuvers caused by the increased horsepower R-2800 development engines that were in the offing. This larger fin and rudder was flight tested at Grumman on F8F-1 (BuNo 94873) and found to be acceptable.

Bureau of Inspection and Survey (BIS) and Fleet Induction Program (FIP) were completed on the F8F-1 Bearcat at NATC Patuxent River, MD, during the middle of 1945. The Bearcat was then deemed acceptable for combat squadrons, which were

about to deploy for the attack on the Japanese mainland.

F8F-1B: With the exception of the first aircraft, all 20mm cannon-armed Bearcats, which had been ordered under the F8F-1C designation, were delivered as F8F-1Bs because the suffix "B" was reassigned in March 1945 to identify Naval aircraft with special armament. Including the aircraft which were initially designated F8F-1C, a total of 226 F8F-1Bs were delivered by Grumman. The first 100 were built interspersed in the F8F-1 production line. The last 126 were built consecutively in two batches before the switch to F8F-2 production, which retained the four cannon armament configuration. The last cannon-equipped aircraft were delivered in August 1947.

F8F-1C: As the Navy was required to perform more and more ground attack missions, consideration was given early in the program to increasing the number of 50 caliber machine guns from four to six. As this could

not be easily accomplished without major modifications to the wing, it was decided that the popular T-31 20mm cannon would solve the problem. Successful trials were performed at Armament Test at NATC Patuxent River, MD, in BuNo 94803 equipped with four T-31 cannon in June 1945. These aircraft were therefore redesignated Bs under the new nomenclature.

F8F-1D: This designation was first applied to BuNo 90456, which was modified in 1949 as a drone cntrol aircraft by the Naval Air Development Center (NADC), Johnsville, PA. Only a few others followed this prototype.

The F8F-1D designation has frequently been used to identify F8F-1s delivered to the French and Thai Air Forces. However, this designation appears to have been unofficial as the use of the suffix "D" did not fit into US Navy Grant-Aid nomenclature at the time. "D" normally indicated conversion of an aircraft to drone control.

F8F-1DB: This unofficial identification had been used, quite possibly in error, to identify cannon-armed F8F-1Bs delivered to the French Armee de l'Air for use in Indochina.

F8F-1E: F8F-1 (BuNo 90445), the ninth production aircraft, was fitted in June of 1945 with an AN/APS-4 radar installed in a radome on a bomb rack beneath the starboard wing to serve as a prototype for a proposed night intruder version. No other Bearcats were fitted or provided with this early radar equipment.

XF8F-1N: In view of the successful adaptation of the Hellcat to the night fighting role, it was logical that a night fighter version of the Bearcat be considered early in the program. Unfortunately, there was not enough space to mount the radome on the inboard leading edge of the wing between the guns and the wing fold. Consequently, the AN/APS-19 had to be installed in a nacelle hung on the bomb rack beneath the starboard wing. Trial installations were made in the summer of 1945 using BuNos 94812 and 94819.

F8F-1N: Twelve F8F-1 airframes were modified to the -N configuration and fitted with the AN/APS-19 radar on the starboard bomb rack during the production cycle at Grumman. Two months later, after the end of the war, it was decided to retain the night fighter role with the well-proven, longer-range Hellcat. Except for further operational testing in the summer of 1945 by VCN-1 and VCN-2, this installation was not adopted for squadron Bearcat service.

F8F-1P: The fifth development Bearcat (BuNo 90441) was modified by the Naval Aircraft Factory in 1946 to evaluate alternative installations of vertical and oblique cameras in the rear fuselage cavity. Because of the production change to the F8F-2, it was decided to produce only F8F-2Ps photographic aircraft.

XF8F-2: The use of the E-series engines with the variable speed hydramatic supercharger and the automatic engine control (AEC) was planned from the onset of the Bearcat program. Pratt and Whitney encountered so many production difficulties with the develoment of that powerplant, that installation of the E-series engines had to be delayed several times. Finally, two development 2,300 HP R-2800-30W E-model engines that had not yet passed their 100 hour, full-power final acceptance tests were installed in F8F-1 Bearcat (BuNo 95049), and in a cannon-equipped F8F-1B airframe (BuNo 95330) which served as the XF8F-2 prototypes. The first flight of XF8F-2 (BuNo 95049) was performed by Carl Alber on 11 June 1947.

F8F-2: The 367 F8F-2s (and prototypes) delivered between November 1947 and April 1949 were powered by the 2250 HP R-2800-34W E-series engines and were fitted with the 12 inch taller fins and rudders which had been tested and approved on BuNo 94873. Even though the "B" suffix was not included in their designation, all of these aircaft were armed with four T-31 20 mm cannon. The F8F-2s had provisions for carrying the same external stores as the late production F8F-1s and -1Bs.

Above, XF8F-1N BuNo 94819 night fighter prototype with its AN/APS-19 on the ground after Pat Gallo had landed it on its 150gal centerline tank at Bethpage. The tank had swiveled from air loads during flight, which prevented the left gear from extending. He landed in the grass alongside the runway and the damage was minimal as the aircraft was flying again three days later. (Grumman) Below, F8F-1 BuNo 95049 became one of two XF8F-2 prototypes. It was later used as a "Dog Ship" at Grumman for any of the continuing Bearcat development tests. (Grumman) Bottom, Corky Meyer in the 63rd F8F-2 BuNo 121612. The -2 a 12" taller fin and rudder, four T-13 20mm cannon as seen on the F8F-1B, and two wing bomb racks with four 5" HVAR rocket stub racks. (Grumman via Corwin Meyer)

Above, F8F-2N BuNo 121601 over Long Island, NY, on 12 August 1948. (H. G. Martin via Jim Hawkins) Below, 121601 was the 7th production F8F-2N and has an AN/APS-19 radar unit fitted on the starboard wing rack. The pilot on this 1 February 1947 test flight was Bill Cochran, who was the radar project test pilot. The 12 F8F-2Ns were used in VC test squadrons. (Grumman) Bottom, Grumman test ship F8F-2N BuNo 121549 "The ESSO B" sans landing gear doors at Grumman Bethpage. (Jim Hawkins via Norm Taylor)

F8F-2D: A few F8F-2s were converted by the Navy as drone directors, and were redesignated F8F-2Ds.

F8F-2N: Twelve F8F-2 airframes were fitted with the AN/APS-19 radar in an underwing pod and were delivered as F8F-2Ns. When they finally ended up in advanced training units at the end of their careers, the radar nacelles were seldom installed and carried.

F8F-2P: The sixty F8F-2Ps delivered by Grumman between February 1948 and May 1949 had the same camera installation developed by the Naval Aircraft Factory in the single F8F-1P in 1946. Their fixed armament was reduced from four to two T-31 20 mm cannon, one in each wing.

F3M-1: Plans in early 1945 were to have General Motors' Eastern Aircraft Division terminate the FM-2 Wildcat production and manufacture the F8F-1 Bearcat under the F3M-1 designation. This was to augment production of Bearcats produced in the Grumman plants. A Letter of Intent for the production of 1876 F3M-1s, which were to be powered by the R-2800-34Ws or -40Ws and armed with four 50 caliber machine guns, was issued in February i945.

The author delivered the thirty-seventh F8F-1 Bearcat (BuNo 94765) to the General Motors Linden, New Jersey, plant on 10 June 1945 to serve as a pattern and pilot checkout aircraft. The General Motors Bearcat contract was canceled at the end of the war before any F3M-1 aircraft were completed.

G-58A: As a replacement for the pre-war Grumman F3F-3 Gulfhawk III biplane, used by demonstration pilot Major Alford 'Al' Williams, the Gulf Oil company ordered a civil version of the F8F-1 in late 1946. All armament and other military equipment was removed and a commercial P&W Double Wasp CA-15 2100 HP eighteen cylinder radial engine was installed. It was registered NL3025 and called the Gulfhawk IV. The author had the privilege of checking this well-known aerobatic pilot out in his new Bearcat in August 1947. He had flown it in only a few demonstrations when a month later he was forced to land it in Elizabeth City, NC, to wait out approaching bad weather. He failed to extend his landing gear and the airplane was completely destroyed by the ensuing fire when his drop tank burst into flames from its contact with the paved runway .

Another G-58A was built to the same specifications as 'Al' Williams'

Gulfhawk IV to replace Hellcats that Roger Wolfe Kahn, the Director of the Grumman Service Department, had used for visiting the many Grumman fighter squadrons located around the country. It had very comprehensive radio and navigation equipment installed and a fixed 150 gallon fuel tank modified to carry spares, tools, or baggage. It was registered N700A. After Roger Kahn's untimely death in 1960, it was subsequently donated to the Cornell University Aeronautical Laboratories for their experimental programs. Several years later it was acquired by William Fornoff. Shortly thereafter it crashed during an airshow.

PUBLIC AIRSHOWS

Being the Bearcat project pilot I was permitted to fly airshows from the first XF8F-1 in 1944 until the arrival of the Grumman Panther jet in 1947. The Bearcat's fantastic takeoff and climb performance, and its high acceleration to maximum speed made airshow demonstrations a great pleasure. Because of the Bearcat's very low lateral stability and more powerful ailerons compared to the Hellcat, I first started performing eight-point slow rolls (or hesitation rolls) in it to please the wartime, aviation-oriented public. A ground observer critic finally gave me good reason to stop showing the Bearcat off with that maneuver.

In early 1946, I was flying a Sunday airshow with Major Alford "Al" Williams. He was still flying his pre-war Grumman F3F-3 biplane fighter and showing his magnificent talents to the thousands of people at the New York Daily Mirror Model Airplane Show at the Grumman Bethpage, New York, airport. I was the last on the list to fly after his skillfully performed aerobatic demonstration. During my time "on stage", I performed two beautiful eight-point rolls and was patting my self on the back because this maneuver was difficult to perform in other aircraft and thus not well known. My wife Dorky was in the audience and she heard a little old lady comment to her friend on my beautiful hesitation roll performance as follows, "I wonder why that pilot

Above, the first F8F-2P BuNo 121580 with Joey Gaeta at the controls on 26 February 1948. The -2Ps had two of the T-31 20mm cannons and ammo removed from their wings to help counterbalance the weight of the three cameras in the aft fuselage. They also had a 25 pound steel balance weight added to the propeller spinner. (Grumman) Below, left-side view of 121580 showing camera port below the forward end of the national insignia. (Grumman) Bottom, Major Al Williams in the cockpit of his Gulfhawk IV Bearcat prior to his first public flight on 11 October 1947. (Grumman)

Above and below, Gulfhawk IV was orange with black and white trim. It is seen here in October 1947 and was only flown until 18 January 1949 when it was destroyed after a gear-up landing and subsequent fire at Bern, NC. (Grumman) Bottom, Grumman's Red Ship N700A was built for the use of Roger Wolfe Kahn, Director of Grumman's Service Dept. (Grumman)

can't roll his airplane smoothly like Mr. Williams did". That was the last eight-point slow roll that I performed after my wife smugly related my audiences' "considered" appreciation of my expertise.

The Great Hellcat-Bearcat Air Show

Soon after the XF8F-1 flew, Mr. Grumman suggested that Pat Gallo and I try to effect a demonstration that would show the performance comparison between the the Bearcat and Hellcat. This was for both Grumman audiences and especially Navy Brass who visited the plant on a regular basis during and after the war.

It began with a full-power formation take-off and climb-out to 3000 feet ending with a 450 mph Bearcat pass down the main runway (see photo page 12). The Bearcat would time his pass to come in from behind and pass the 350 mph Hellcat in the middle of the airfield where the audience waited. At the end of the runway both aircraft would then pull-up in a 5G vertical climb until the Bearcat was out of sight. It made the Bearcat's performance stand out beautifully in relation to the Hellcat because both aircraft had Pratt and Whitney R-2800 2000 horsepower engines.

The standing start, take-off and climb-out were easy to perform together and showed a magnificent difference in performance abilities of the two aircraft. With the Hellcat being much slower accelerating to its high speed at sea level, timing to get both aircraft to pass the audience at the middle of the field proved most difficult. We tried many times and many ways but we didn't seem to be able to satisfy ourselves, or Mr. Grumman, in

our practice airshows.

We finally decided to pick two large buildings in line with the runway, one about three miles from the field and the other five miles away, to begin our full-power runs simultaneously. I started my run to the Grumman airport in the slower Hellcat over the three mile building and Pat started his at the five mile one. This system worked every time. Neither of us could fathom why it worked, but he always passed me right over the audience location at the mid-field Grumman runway with over a hundred miles-per-hour speed differential. The Bearcat always disappeared into the sky in his vertical climb-out

Above, N700A after being returned to service after being purchased by William Fornoff. (Grumman) Below, Fornoff bought a second ship registered as N7700C and he and his son Corky flew the aircraft together until a mid-air which fatally injured Bill Fornoff. These ships were red with black trim bordered by yellow. (Grumman and via Norm Taylor)

while I had to loop precariously out of my vertical climb at about three thousand feet. We were called-on to perform this airshow many times. We had as much fun as the people watching.

F8F MODEL COMPARISONS

	XF8F-1	F8F-1	F8F-1B	F8F-1N	F8F-2	F8F-2N	F8F-2P
1st Flight	08/31/44		02/12/46	05/13/46	06/11/47	11/21/47	02/20/48
Test Pilot	Hall	Seligman	Gallo	Alber	Gallo	Ritchie	Meyer
1st Delivery	2/26/45	12/30/44	02/27/46	05/29/46	10/11/47	12/22/47	02/26/48
Last Delivery		08/29/47	01/28/48	11/12/46	04/14/49	04/22/49	05/31/49
Powerplant	R-2800-22W	R-2800-34W	R-2800-34W	R-2800-34W	R-2800-30W	R-2800-30W	R-2800-30W
Propeller	Aeroproducts 4-blade 12'7" diameter (all)						
Armament	4-.50cal	4-.50cal	4-20mm	4-.50cal	4-20mm	4-20mm	2-20mm
Span, Wing	35'6"	35'6"	35'6"	35'6"	35'6"	35'6"	35'6"
Span Folded	23'3"	23'3"	23'3"	23'3"	23'3"	23'3"	23'3"
Airfoil Section	At Fuselage NACA 23018, at Construction Tip NACA 23009						
Chord at Root	115.87"	115.87"	115.87"	115.87"	115.87"	115.87"	115.87"
Chord at Tip	51.5"	51.5"	51.5"	51.5"	51.5"	51.5"	51.5"
Wing Incidence	1.5°	1.5°	1.5°	1.5°	1.5°	1.5°	1.5°
Wing Dihedral	5° 30'	5° 30'	5° 30'	5° 30'	5° 30'	5° 30'	5° 30'
Sweep Back	5° 5'	5° 5'	5° 5'	5° 5'	5° 5'	5° 5'	5° 5'
Length	27'6"	27'6"	27'6"	27'6"	27'6"	27'6"	27'6"
Length on Gear	28'3"	28'3"	28'3"	28'3"	28'3"	28'3"	28'3"
Height on Gear	13'8"	13'8"	13'8"	13'8"	13'8"	13'8"	13'8"
Max Fus. Width	56"	56"	56"	56"	56"	56"	56"
Max Fus. Height	80"	80"	80"	80"	80"	80"	80"
Fus. Length	248"	248"	248"	248"	248"	248"	248"
Length w/Engine	291"	291"	291"	291"	291"	291"	291"
Stabilizer Span	189"	189"	189"	189"	189"	189"	189"
Stab. Incidence	1/2°	1/2°	1/2°	1/2°	1/2°	1/2°	1/2°
Areas: Wings	244sq.ft.	244sq.ft.	244sq.ft.	244sq.ft.	244sq.ft.	244sq.ft.	244sq.ft.
Flaps	18.18sq.ft.	18.18sq.ft.	18.18sq.ft.	18.18sq.ft.	18.18sq.ft.	18.18sq.ft.	18.18sq.ft.
Ailerons	20.7sq.ft.	20.7sq.ft.	20.7sq.ft.	20.7sq.ft.	20.7sq.ft.	20.7sq.ft.	20.7sq.ft.
Stabilizer & Elev.	52.27sq.ft.	52.27sq.ft.	52.27sq.ft.	52.27sq.ft.	52.27sq.ft.	52.27sq.ft.	52.27sq.ft.
Elevators & Tabs	18.63sq.ft.	18.63sq.ft.	18.63sq.ft.	18.63sq.ft.	18.63sq.ft.	18.63sq.ft.	18.63sq.ft.
Elev. Trim Tabs	1.4sq.ft.	1.4sq.ft.	1.4sq.ft.	1.4sq.ft.	1.4sq.ft.	1.4sq.ft.	1.4sq.ft.
Vertical Fin	20.8sq.ft.	20.8sq.ft.	20.8sq.ft.	20.8sq.ft.	22.5sq.ft.	22.5sq.ft.	22.5sq.ft.
Rudder & Tab	8.1sq.ft.	8.1sq.ft.	8.1sq.ft.	8.1sq.ft.	8.16sq.ft.	8.16sq.ft.	8.16sq.ft.
Rudder Tab	.6sq,ft.	.6sq,ft.	.6sq,ft.	.6sq,ft.	.88sq,ft.	.88sq,ft.	.88sq,ft.
Weight Empty	7,017lbs	7,170lbs	7,216lbs	7,510lbs	7,650	7,775	8,125
Weight Combat	8,116lbs	9,334lbs	9,672lbs	9,770lbs	10,337	10,100	10.080
VMAX Sea Level	425	391	366	388	336	332	334
VMAX Crit. Alt.	455	429	372	419	388	385	388
Max Climb fpm	6,500	5,600	5,610	5,550	4,465	4,360	4,570
Max Range Ferry	1,450	1,965	1,810	1,895	1,595	1,586	1,595
Service Ceiling	41,300	38,900	34,800	34,900	38,200	40,500	38,350
Internal Fuel	162gals	185gals	185gals	185gals	185gals	185gals	185gals

At left, the one-off F8F-1E BuNo 90445 on 22 June 1945 with an AN/APS-5 radome wing pod mounted under the right wing. (Grumman via Corwin Meyer) Above, F8F-1 BuNo 94765 on bailment to the Aeroproducts Propeller Company with Aeroproducts Flight Test logo on the engine cowl. Note taped wingtip breakaway joint. (Ginter collection)

PRODUCTION SEQUENCE:

2	XF8F-1	BuNos 90460-90461
23	F8F-1	Pre-production aircraft BuNos 90437-90459; 90456 became prototype F8F-1D

Conversions:

1		F8F-1D prototype BuNo 90456
		F8F-1D BuNos 90446, 90447, 90451-90457
747	F8F-1	BuNos 94752-95498 (original contract was for 2000 F8F-1s)

Conversions:

1		F8F-1C prototype BuNo 94803
1		F8F-1B prototype BuNo 94972
98		F8F-1B BuNos 94982/94987/94999/95002/95009/95015/95022/95028/95033/95039/95044/95050/95056/95062/ 95068/95074/95080/95086/95093/95098/95103/95108/95113/95118/95123/95128/95133/95138/95143/95148/ 95156/95162/95166/95172/95176/95181/95190/95195/95200/95205/95210/95215/95221/95227/95232/95237/ 95242/95247/95253/95260/95265/95271/95275/95281/95285/95290/95295/95300/95305/95310/95315/95319/ 95324/95334/95340/95344/95349/95354/95359/95363/95368/95373/95378/95383/95387/95391/95396/95401/ 95406/95411/95416/95420/95425/95430/95435/95440/95445/95450/95454/95459/95463/95468/95472/95477/ 95482/95487/95492/95498
		F8F-1D BuNos 94752/95009/95325/95342
1		F8F-1E BuNo 90445
2		F8F-1N prototype BuNo 94812/94819
12		F8F-1N BuNos 95034/95140/95150/95161/05171/95182/95191/95198/95206/95214/95222/95230
1		F8F-1P prototype BuNo 90441
2		XF8F-2 prototype BuNos 95049-95330
126	F8F-1B	BuNos 121463-121522/122087-122152
270	F8F-2	BuNos 121523-121792
95	F8F-2	BuNos 122614-122708

Conversions:

1		F8F-2N prototype 121549
12		F8F-2N BuNos 121549-121550/121575-121579/121601-121605
1		F8F-2P prototype 121580
60		F8F-2P BuNos 121580-121585/121606-121611/121632-121637/121658-121663/121684-121689/121709-121714/ 121734-121739/121753-121758/121770-121775/121785-121790
		F8F-2D known BuNos 121698/121704/121716/121724-725/121782/121784/122663/122672/122690

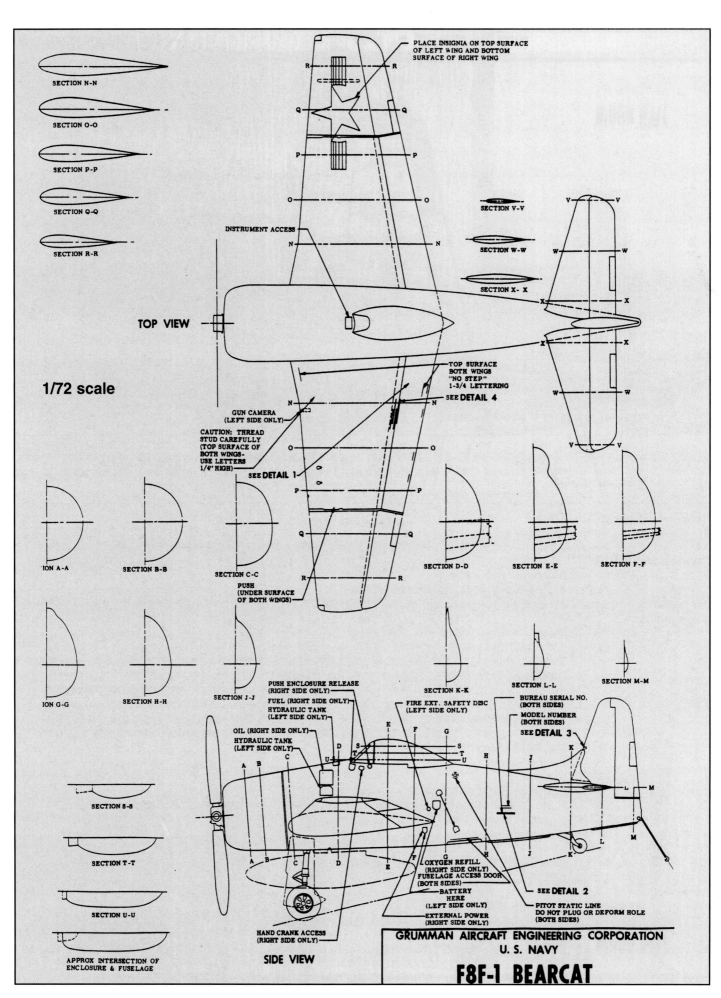

SECTION N-N

SECTION O-O

SECTION P-P

SECTION Q-Q

SECTION R-R

1/72 scale

TOP VIEW

PLACE INSIGNIA ON TOP SURFACE
OF LEFT WING AND BOTTOM
SURFACE OF RIGHT WING

SECTION V-V

SECTION W-W

SECTION X-X

INSTRUMENT ACCESS

TOP SURFACE
BOTH WINGS
"NO STEP"
1-3/4 LETTERING
SEE DETAIL 4

GUN CAMERA
(LEFT SIDE ONLY)

CAUTION: THREAD
STUD CAREFULLY
(TOP SURFACE OF
BOTH WINGS-
USE LETTERS
1/4" HIGH)
SEE DETAIL 1

PUSH
(UNDER SURFACE
OF BOTH WINGS)

ION A-A

SECTION B-B

SECTION C-C

SECTION D-D

SECTION E-E

SECTION F-F

ION G-G

SECTION H-H

SECTION J-J

SECTION K-K

SECTION L-L

SECTION M-M

PUSH ENCLOSURE RELEASE
(RIGHT SIDE ONLY)

FUEL (RIGHT SIDE ONLY)

HYDRAULIC TANK
(LEFT SIDE ONLY)

OIL (RIGHT SIDE ONLY)

HYDRAULIC TANK
(LEFT SIDE ONLY)

FIRE EXT. SAFETY DISC
(LEFT SIDE ONLY)

BUREAU SERIAL NO.
(BOTH SIDES)

MODEL NUMBER
(BOTH SIDES)
SEE DETAIL 3

SECTION S-S

SECTION T-T

SECTION U-U

APPROX INTERSECTION OF
ENCLOSURE & FUSELAGE

HAND CRANK ACCESS
(RIGHT SIDE ONLY)

SIDE VIEW

OXYGEN REFILL
(RIGHT SIDE ONLY)
FUSELAGE ACCESS DOOR
(BOTH SIDES)

BATTERY
HERE
(LEFT SIDE ONLY)

EXTERNAL POWER
(RIGHT SIDE ONLY)

SEE DETAIL 2

PITOT STATIC LINE
DO NOT PLUG OR DEFORM HOLE
(BOTH SIDES)

GRUMMAN AIRCRAFT ENGINEERING CORPORATION
U. S. NAVY
F8F-1 BEARCAT

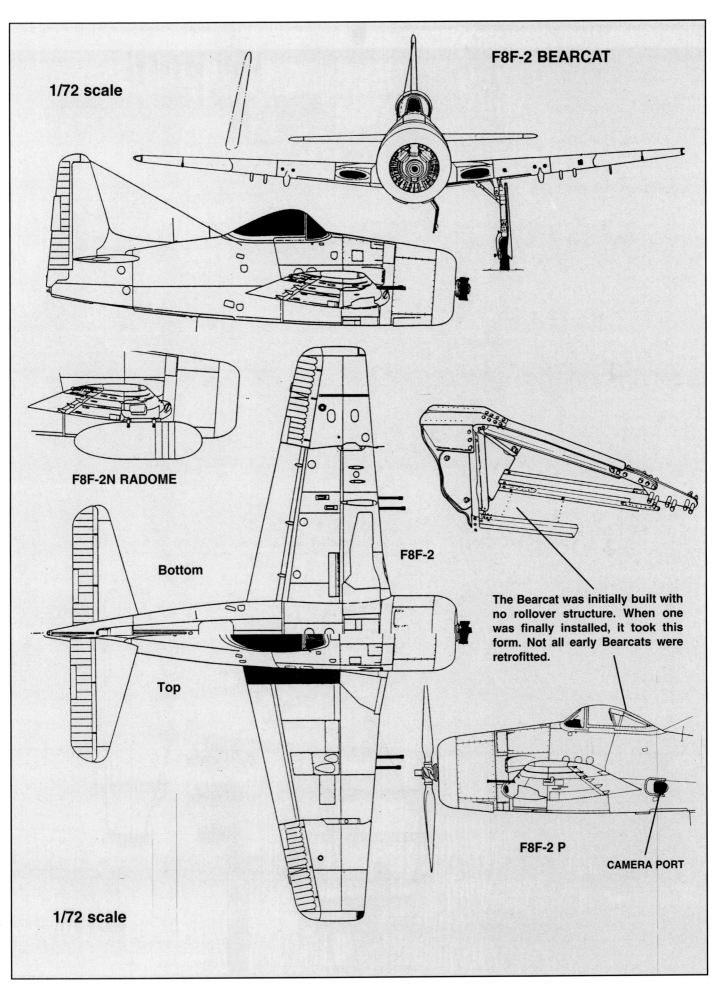

F8F-2 BEARCAT

1/72 scale

F8F-2N RADOME

Bottom

Top

F8F-2

The Bearcat was initially built with no rollover structure. When one was finally installed, it took this form. Not all early Bearcats were retrofitted.

F8F-2 P

CAMERA PORT

1/72 scale

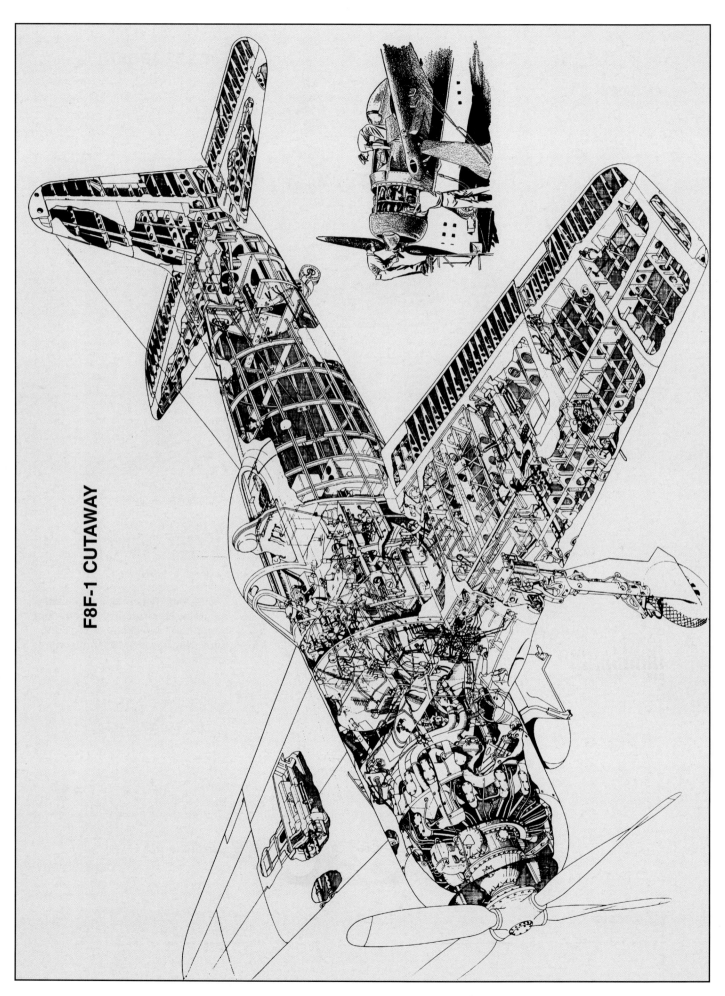

F8F-1 CUTAWAY

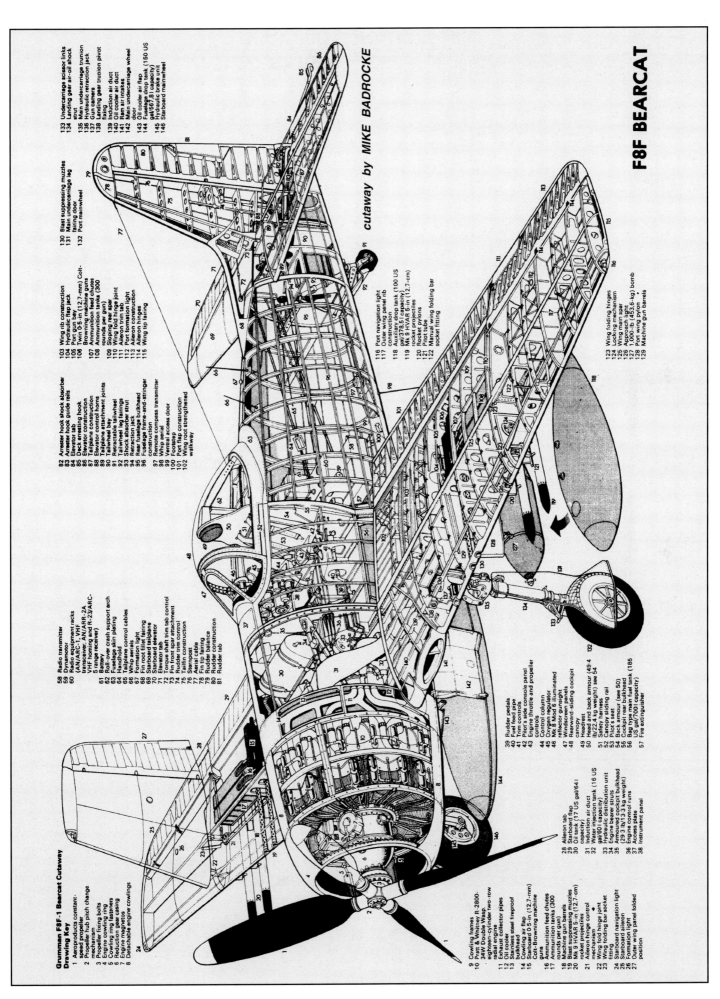

F8F BEARCAT

cutaway by MIKE BADROCKE

Grumman F8F-1 Bearcat Cutaway Drawing Key

1 Aeroproducts constant-speed propeller
2 Propeller hub pitch change mechanism
3 Propeller fixing bolts
4 Engine cowling ring
5 Cowling ring fasteners
6 Reduction gear casing
7 Engine magnetos
8 Detachable engine cowlings
9 Cowling frames
10 Pratt & Whitney R-2800-34W Double Wasp, eighteen-cylinder two-row radial engine
11 Exhaust collector pipes
12 Oil cooler
13 Stainless steel fireproof bulkhead
14 Cowling air flap
15 Starboard 0·5-in (12·7-mm) Colt-Browning machine guns
16 Ammunition feed chutes
17 Ammunition tanks (300 rounds per gun)
18 Machine gun barrels
19 Blast suppressing muzzles
20 Mk 9 HVAR 5-in (12·7-cm) rocket projectiles
21 Aileron hinge control mechanism
22 Wing fold hinge joint
23 Wing folding bar socket fitting
24 Starboard navigation light
25 Starboard aileron
26 Formation light
27 Outer wing panel folded position
28 Aileron tab
29 Machine gun barrels
30 Starboard flap
31 Induction air duct
32 Water injection tank (16 US gal/60 l capacity)
33 Hydraulic distribution unit
34 Oil tank (17 US gal/64·l capacity)
35 Engine bearer struts
36 Armoured cockpit bulkhead (29·3 lb/13·3 kg weight)
37 Engine control runs
38 Instrument panel
39 Rudder pedals
40 Fuel feed pipe
41 Trim controls
42 Pilot's side console panel
43 Engine throttle and propeller controls
44 Controls
45 Control column
46 Oxygen regulator
47 Mk 8 Mod 6 illuminated reflector gunsight
48 Windscreen panels
49 Headrest
50 Head and back armour (49·4 lb/22·4 kg weight) see 54
51 Safety harness
52 Canopy sliding rail
53 Pilot's seat
54 Back armour (see 50)
55 Cockpit rear bulkhead
56 Bag type main fuel tank (185 US gal/700 l capacity)
57 Fire extinguisher
58 Radio transmitter
59 Dynamotor
60 Radio equipment racks (AN/ARC-1, VHF transceiver; AN/ARR-2A VHF homing and R-23/ARC-B range receiver)
61 Battery
62 Roll-over crash support arch
63 Fuselage skin plating
64 Handhold
65 Tailplane control cables
66 Whip aerials
67 Port formation light
68 Fin root fillet fairing
69 Starboard tailplane
70 Starboard elevator
71 Elevator tab
72 Torque shaft trim tab control
73 Fin front spar attachment
74 Rudder trim control
75 Tailfin construction
76 Sternpost
77 Fin tip fairing
78 Rudder balance
79 Rudder construction
80 Rudder construction
81 Rudder tab
82 Arrester hook shock absorber
83 Arrester hook guide rails
84 Elevator tab
85 Deck arresting hook
86 Elevator construction
87 Tailplane construction
88 Elevator control horns
89 Tailplane attachment joints
90 Tailwheel bay
91 Retractable tailwheel
92 Tailwheel leg hinge joint
93 Shock absorber strut
94 Retraction jack
95 Rear fuselage bulkhead construction
96 Rear fuselage frame-and-stringer construction
97 Remote compass transmitter
98 Whip aerial
99 Ventral access door
100 Footstep
101 Tailfin root construction
102 Wing root strengthened walkway
103 Wing rib construction
104 Hydraulic flap jack
105 Main undercarriage leg
106 Twin 0·5-in (12·7-mm) Colt-Browning machine guns
107 Ammunition feed chutes
108 Ammunition tanks (300 rounds per gun)
109 Wingtip mast
110 Wing fold hinge joint
111 Aileron trim tab
112 Port formation light
113 Aileron construction
114 Aileron hinges
115 Wing tip fairing
116 Port navigation light
117 Outer wing panel rib construction
118 Auxiliary drop tank (100 US gal/378·5 l capacity)
119 Mk 9 HVAR 5-in (12·7-cm) rocket projectiles
120 Rocket pylons
121 Pitot tube
122 Manual wing folding bar socket fitting
123 Wing folding hinges
124 Locking mechanism
125 Wing main spar
126 Approach light
127 1,000-lb (453·6-kg) bomb
128 Port wing pylon
129 Machine gun barrels
130 Blast suppressing muzzles
131 Main undercarriage leg
132 Port mainwheel
133 Undercarriage scissor links
134 Landing gear air-oil shock strut
135 Main undercarriage trunion
136 Hydraulic retraction jack
137 Gun camera
138 Landing gear trunion pivot fixing
139 Induction air duct
140 Oil cooler air duct
141 Ram air intakes
142 Main undercarriage wheel door
143 Oil cooler air flap
144 Fuselage drop tank (150 US gal/568 l capacity)
145 Hydraulic brake unit
146 Starboard mainwheel

31

F8F STATIONS DIAGRAM

NOT TO SCALE

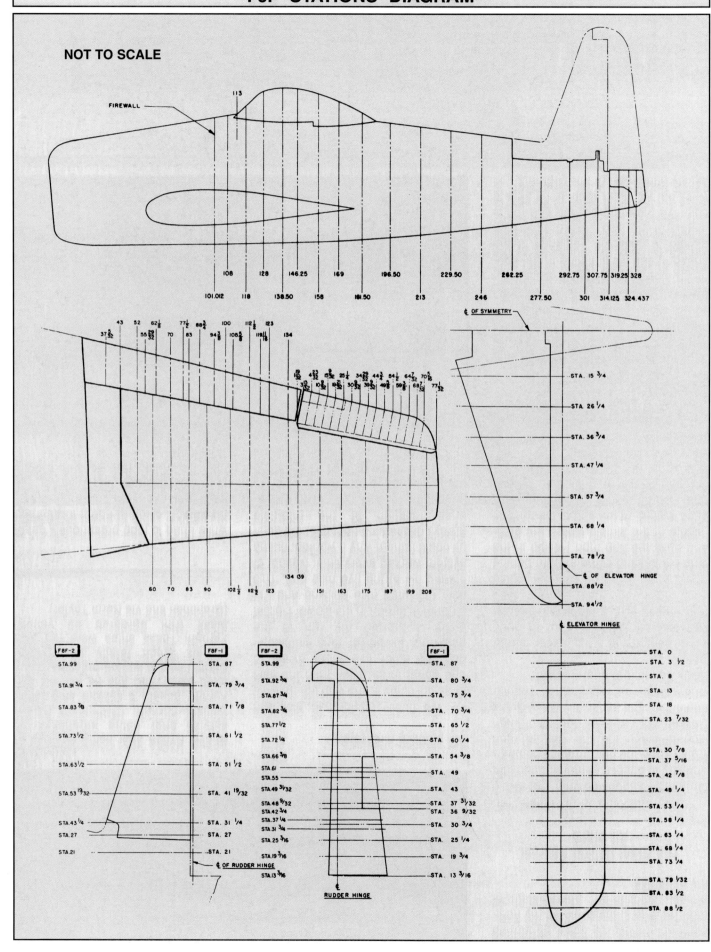

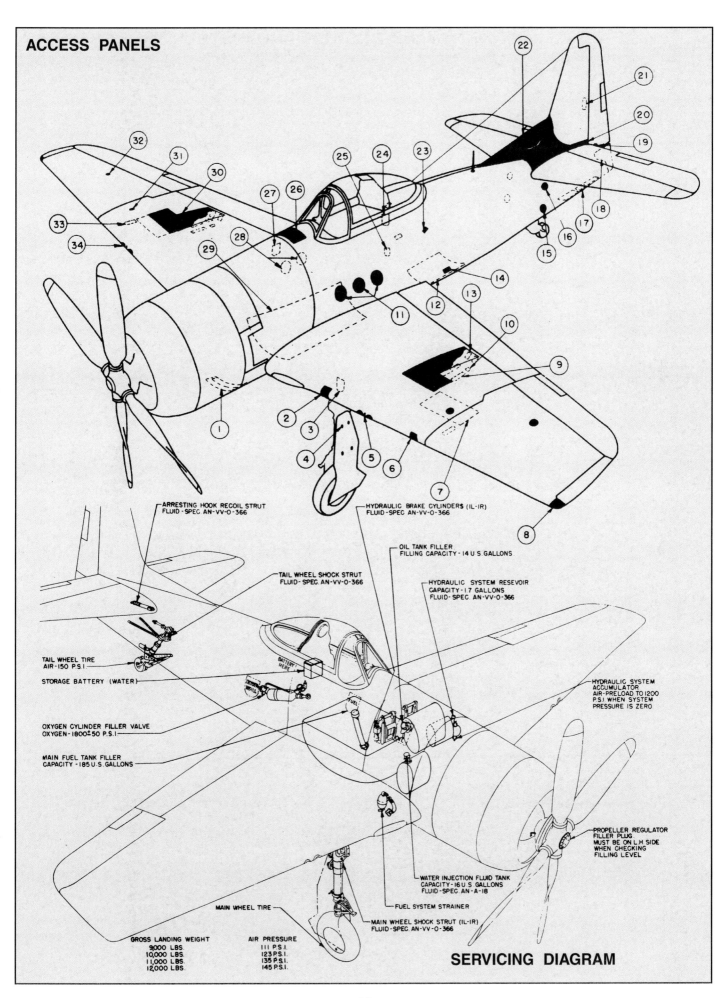

ACCESS PANELS

ARRESTING HOOK RECOIL STRUT
FLUID - SPEC AN-VV-O-366

TAIL WHEEL SHOCK STRUT
FLUID - SPEC. AN-VV-O-366

HYDRAULIC BRAKE CYLINDERS (IL-IR)
FLUID - SPEC AN-VV-O-366

OIL TANK FILLER.
FILLING CAPACITY - 14 U.S.GALLONS.

HYDRAULIC SYSTEM RESEVOIR
CAPACITY - 1.7 GALLONS
FLUID- SPEC. AN-VV-O-366

TAIL WHEEL TIRE
AIR - 150 P.S.I.

STORAGE BATTERY (WATER)

HYDRAULIC SYSTEM
ACCUMULATOR
AIR-PRELOAD TO 1200
P.S.I. WHEN SYSTEM
PRESSURE IS ZERO

OXYGEN CYLINDER FILLER VALVE
OXYGEN - 1800±50 P.S.I

MAIN FUEL TANK FILLER
CAPACITY - 185 U.S. GALLONS.

PROPELLER REGULATOR
FILLER PLUG.
MUST BE ON L.H. SIDE
WHEN CHECKING
FILLING LEVEL

WATER INJECTION FLUID TANK
CAPACITY - 16 U.S GALLONS
FLUID - SPEC. AN-A-18

MAIN WHEEL TIRE

FUEL SYSTEM STRAINER

MAIN WHEEL SHOCK STRUT (IL-IR)
FLUID - SPEC. AN-VV-O-366

GROSS LANDING WEIGHT	AIR PRESSURE
9,000 LBS.	111 P.S.I.
10,000 LBS.	123 P.S.I.
11,000 LBS.	135 P.S.I.
12,000 LBS.	145 P.S.I.

SERVICING DIAGRAM

F8F-1/-1B
FORWARD COCKPIT
AND
INSTRUMENT PANEL

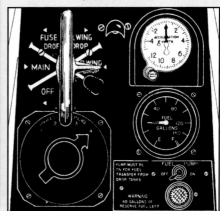

Below, fuel controls.

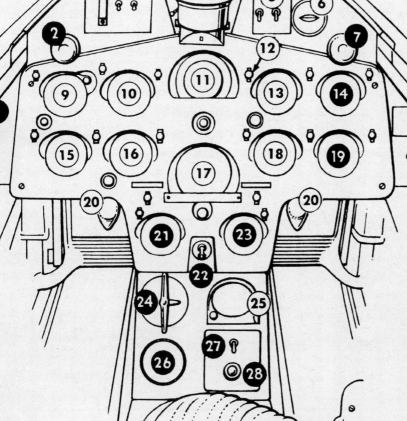

1. Ignition Switch
2. Supercharger Control
3. Armament Master and Gun Switches
4. Gun Sight
5. Bomb, Tank and R. P. Switches
6. Oxgyen Flow Indicator
7. Carburetor Air Control
8. Landing Gear Emergency Control
9. Clock
10. Airspeed Indicator
11. Attitude Gyro Indicator
12. Panel Lights
13. Compass Indicator
14. Manifold Pressure Gage

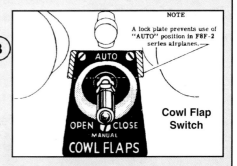

NOTE

A lock plate prevents use of "AUTO" position in F8F-2 series airplanes.

Cowl Flap Switch

15. Rocket Selector
16. Altimeter
17. Directional Gyro
18. Turn and Bank Indicator
19. Tachometer
20. Gun Charging Controls
21. Engine Gage Unit
22. Cowl Flaps Switch
23. Cyinder Head Temperature Gage
24. Fuel Tank Selector Valve
25. Accelerometer
26. Fuel Quantity Gage
27. Auxiliary Fuel Pump Switch
28. Fuel Reserve Warning Light

BEARCAT CANOPY AND CANOPY CONTROLS

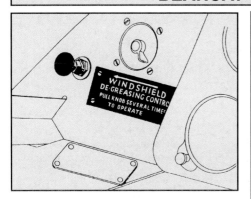

Above, windscreen degreasing control. Below, outside canopy release. At right, three views of the canopy prior to roll-over structure being installed. (USN)

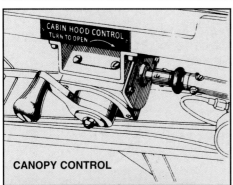

CANOPY CONTROL

PILOT'S SEAT

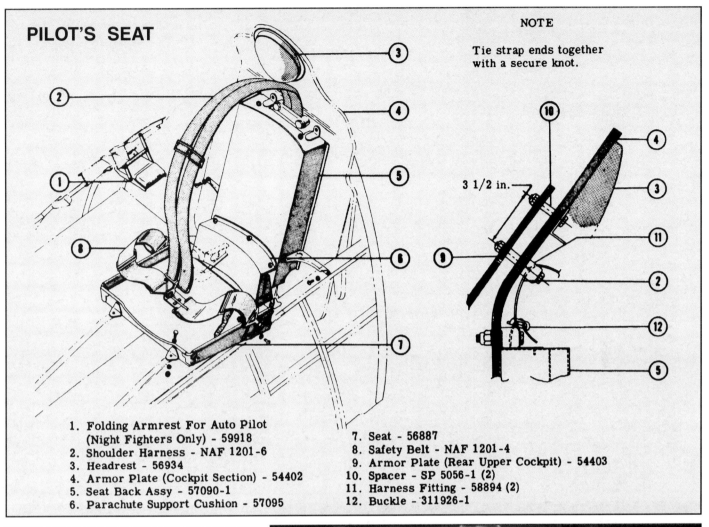

NOTE

Tie strap ends together with a secure knot.

3 1/2 in.

1. Folding Armrest For Auto Pilot (Night Fighters Only) - 59918
2. Shoulder Harness - NAF 1201-6
3. Headrest - 56934
4. Armor Plate (Cockpit Section) - 54402
5. Seat Back Assy - 57090-1
6. Parachute Support Cushion - 57095
7. Seat - 56887
8. Safety Belt - NAF 1201-4
9. Armor Plate (Rear Upper Cockpit) - 54403
10. Spacer - SP 5056-1 (2)
11. Harness Fitting - 58894 (2)
12. Buckle - 311926-1

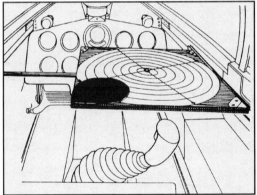

Above, pilot's chartboard deployed. Below, surface control locks in place. The pilot's lap belt was used as part of this system.

G-16748
2-26-45

XF8F-1 LEFT-HAND PILOT'S CONSOLE

F8F-1 LEFT-HAND PILOT'S CONSOLE

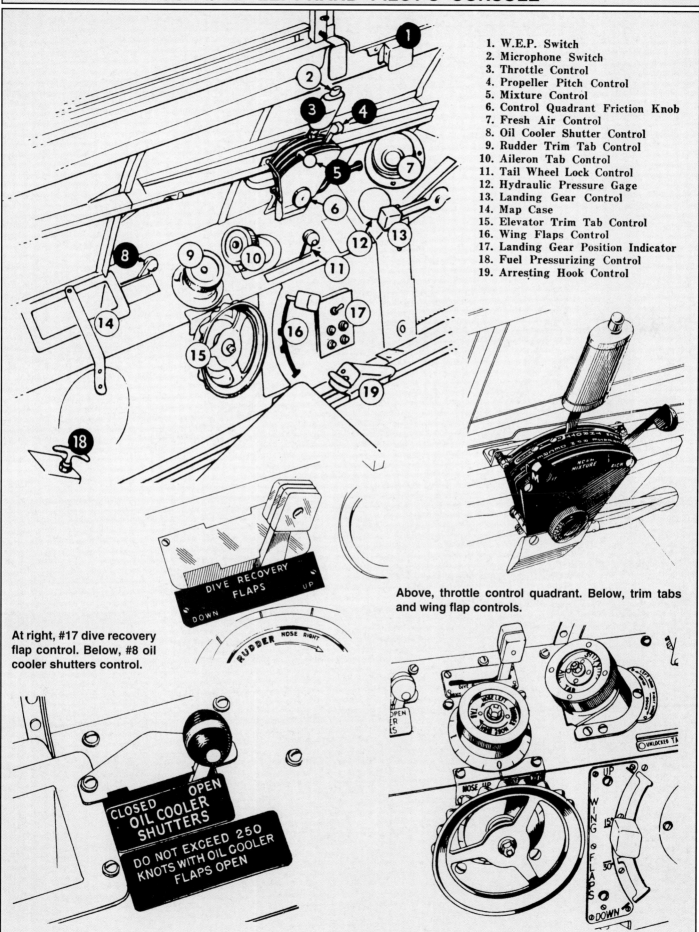

1. W.E.P. Switch
2. Microphone Switch
3. Throttle Control
4. Propeller Pitch Control
5. Mixture Control
6. Control Quadrant Friction Knob
7. Fresh Air Control
8. Oil Cooler Shutter Control
9. Rudder Trim Tab Control
10. Aileron Tab Control
11. Tail Wheel Lock Control
12. Hydraulic Pressure Gage
13. Landing Gear Control
14. Map Case
15. Elevator Trim Tab Control
16. Wing Flaps Control
17. Landing Gear Position Indicator
18. Fuel Pressurizing Control
19. Arresting Hook Control

DIVE RECOVERY FLAPS
UP
DOWN

RUDDER NOSE RIGHT

Above, throttle control quadrant. Below, trim tabs and wing flap controls.

At right, #17 dive recovery flap control. Below, #8 oil cooler shutters control.

CLOSED   OPEN
OIL COOLER SHUTTERS
DO NOT EXCEED 250 KNOTS WITH OIL COOLER FLAPS OPEN

1. Cockpit Canopy Control
2. Hand Microphone
3. Oxygen Gage
4. Oxygen Regulator
5. Voltmeter
6. Electrical Distribution Panel
7. Fresh Air Control
8. Electrical Distribution Panel
9. Radio Control Panel
10. Radio Destructor Switch
11. Microphone Jack
12. Circuit Breaker Panel
13. Hydraulic Hand Pump
14. Hand Pump Selector Valve
15. Oxygen Tank Valve Control

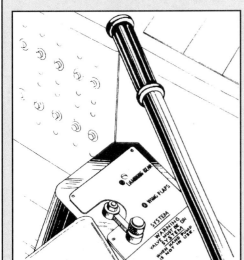

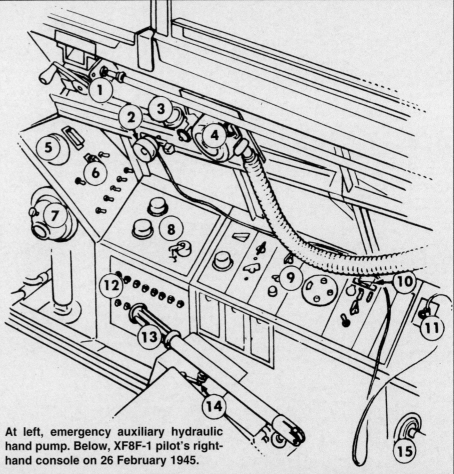

At left, emergency auxiliary hydraulic hand pump. Below, XF8F-1 pilot's right-hand console on 26 February 1945.

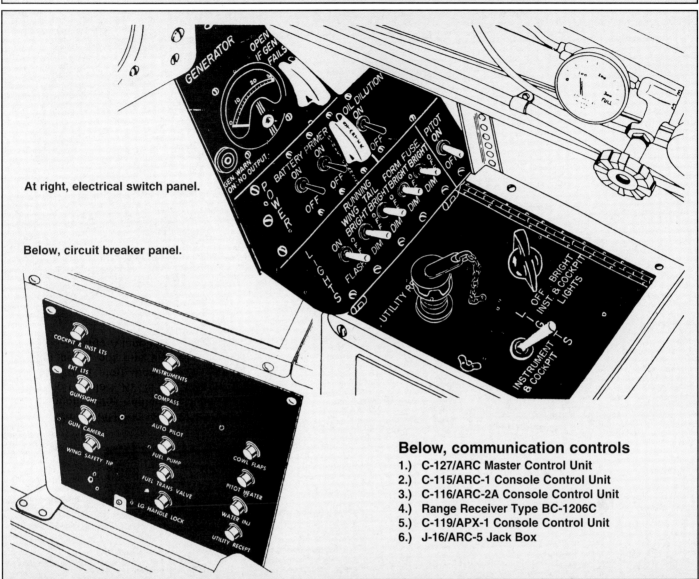

At right, electrical switch panel.

Below, circuit breaker panel.

Below, communication controls
1.) C-127/ARC Master Control Unit
2.) C-115/ARC-1 Console Control Unit
3.) C-116/ARC-2A Console Control Unit
4.) Range Receiver Type BC-1206C
5.) C-119/APX-1 Console Control Unit
6.) J-16/ARC-5 Jack Box

F8F-1N COCKPIT LAYOUT

COCKPIT EMERGENCY CONTROLS

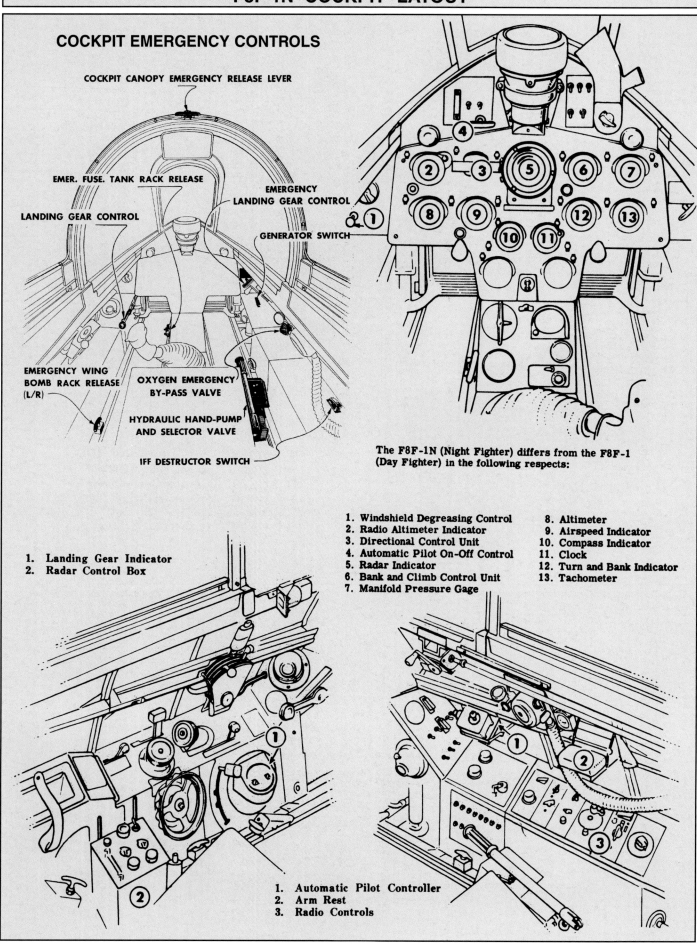

COCKPIT CANOPY EMERGENCY RELEASE LEVER

EMER. FUSE. TANK RACK RELEASE

EMERGENCY LANDING GEAR CONTROL

LANDING GEAR CONTROL

GENERATOR SWITCH

EMERGENCY WING BOMB RACK RELEASE (L/R)

OXYGEN EMERGENCY BY-PASS VALVE

HYDRAULIC HAND-PUMP AND SELECTOR VALVE

IFF DESTRUCTOR SWITCH

The F8F-1N (Night Fighter) differs from the F8F-1 (Day Fighter) in the following respects:

1. Windshield Degreasing Control
2. Radio Altimeter Indicator
3. Directional Control Unit
4. Automatic Pilot On-Off Control
5. Radar Indicator
6. Bank and Climb Control Unit
7. Manifold Pressure Gage

8. Altimeter
9. Airspeed Indicator
10. Compass Indicator
11. Clock
12. Turn and Bank Indicator
13. Tachometer

1. Landing Gear Indicator
2. Radar Control Box

1. Automatic Pilot Controller
2. Arm Rest
3. Radio Controls

F8F-2/-2N/2P COCKPIT LAYOUT

1. Ignition Switch.
2. Supercharger Control (Removed when AEC Unit is Installed).
3. Armament Master and Fire Control Switches.
4. Gun Sight.
5. Bomb and Tank Selector Switches.
6. Winshield Defogger.
7. Protected Carburetor Air Control.
8. Landing Gear Emergency Control.
9. Radio Altimeter.
10. Low Limit Light--Radio Altimeter.
11. Airspeed Indicator.
12. Gyro Horizon Indicator (Radar Indicator-2N Only).
13. Panel Lights
14. Rate of Climb Indicator.
15. Manifold Pressure Gage
16. Altimeter.
17. Compass Indicator or G-2 Compass Control Switch.
18. Directional Gyro or G-2 Compass Indicator.
19. Turn and Bank Indicator.
20. Tachometer.
21. Cannon Charging Controls.
22. Engine Gage Unit.
23. Cowl Flaps Switch.
24. Cylinder Head Temperature Gage.
25. Fuel Tank Selector Valve.
26. Accelerometer.
27. Rocket Selector Switch.
28. Auxiliary Fuel Pump Switch.
29. Fuel Quantity Gage.
30. Fuel Reserve Warning Light.
31. Emergency Release Fuselage Tank.
32. Trigger--Cannons.
33. Trigger--Bombs, Tanks.
34. Trigger--Rockets.
35. Auto Pilot On-Off Control-2N Only.

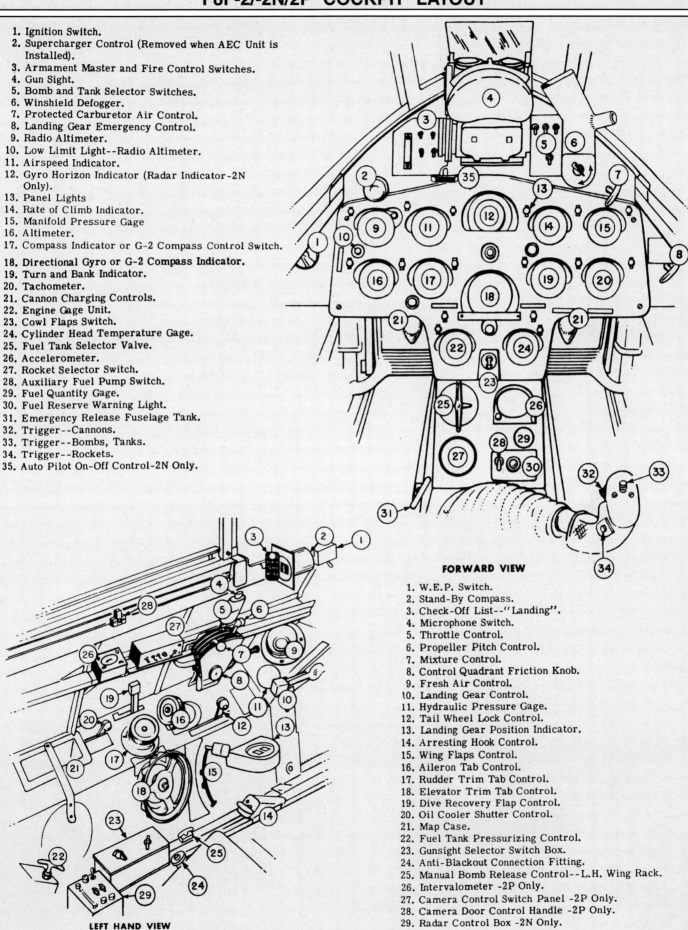

FORWARD VIEW

1. W.E.P. Switch.
2. Stand-By Compass.
3. Check-Off List--"Landing".
4. Microphone Switch.
5. Throttle Control.
6. Propeller Pitch Control.
7. Mixture Control.
8. Control Quadrant Friction Knob.
9. Fresh Air Control.
10. Landing Gear Control.
11. Hydraulic Pressure Gage.
12. Tail Wheel Lock Control.
13. Landing Gear Position Indicator.
14. Arresting Hook Control.
15. Wing Flaps Control.
16. Aileron Tab Control.
17. Rudder Trim Tab Control.
18. Elevator Trim Tab Control.
19. Dive Recovery Flap Control.
20. Oil Cooler Shutter Control.
21. Map Case.
22. Fuel Tank Pressurizing Control.
23. Gunsight Selector Switch Box.
24. Anti-Blackout Connection Fitting.
25. Manual Bomb Release Control--L.H. Wing Rack.
26. Intervalometer -2P Only.
27. Camera Control Switch Panel -2P Only.
28. Camera Door Control Handle -2P Only.
29. Radar Control Box -2N Only.

LEFT HAND VIEW

RIGHT HAND VIEW

1. Clock-Eight Day.
2. Check-Off List--"Take Off".
3. Cockpit Sliding Canopy Control.
4. Oxygen Pressure Gage.
5. Oxygen Regulator.
6. Oxygen Flow Indicator.
7. Chartboard Rail.
8. Voltmeter.
9. Electrical Distribution Panel.
10. Fresh Air Control.
11. Radio Control Panel.
12. IFF Destruction Switch.
13. Radio Altitude Limit Switch.
14. Circuit Breaker Panel.
15. Hydraulic Hand Pump.
16. Hand Pump Selector.
17. Oxygen Tank Valve Early Models Only.
18. Manual Bomb Release Control--R.H. Wing Rack.
19. Canopy Open Lock Release.
20. Auto Pilot Controller.

At left, F8F-2 istrument panel. Below left,
F8F-2 left-hand console.

OXYGEN SYSTEM

1. Flow Indicator
2. Pressure Gage
3. Oxygen Regulator
4. Air Dilution Valve
5. Mask
6. Oxygen Bottle
7. Filler Valve
8. Shut-off Valve
9. Breather Tube
10. Diaphragm Knob
11. Emergency By-pass Valve

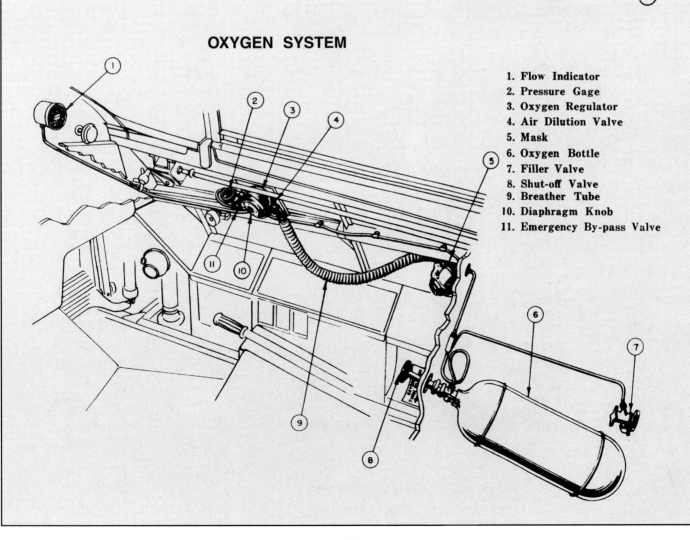

F8F--2N GUNSIGHT AND INSTRUMENT PANEL

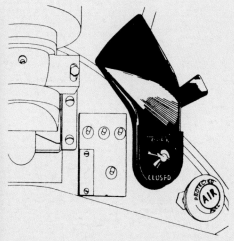

Above, defogging duct and control switch. At right, automatic pilot on-off control was located below the left-hand armament panel located at the top of the instrument panel.

Above, F8F-2N gunsight and instrument hood with defogging duct on the right side. Bottom, F8F-2N instrument panel with radar scope in the center. (USN)

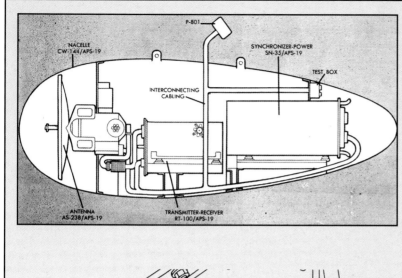

F8F-2N EQUIPMENT AND LEFT-HAND CONSOLE

At left, APS-19 wing pod arrangement. Below, automatic pilot controller on F8F-2N was located above the right forward console. The autopilot was unique to the F8F-1N and F8F-2N. A GR-1 unit was used on the -1N and the GR-2 on the -2N. Bottom, F8F-2N left-hand console with radar control at left bottom.

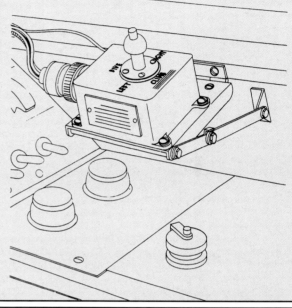

Very large APS-19 radar pod with its bulky connector viewed from behind while mounted on the right wing of an F8F-2N. Below, right-hand view of the APS-19 pod. Note length of the 20mm cannon barrels and the flared muzzle flash suppressors. (National Archives)

G-32448

G-32447

The F8F-2P's electrical control panel was located on the left-hand side of the cockpit adjacent to the intervalometer. It contained the master camera switch, manual and automatic switches, and the camera system warning lights. The film feed warning light and the camera door light were green and the intervalometer light was red.

The controls for the B-3B type intervalometer consisted of the power supply toggle switch, setting knob, recycle knob, and an extra-picture switch. The dial on the top of the intervalometer was graduated in seconds for the direct indication of the time interval between film exposures. A setting hand indicated the selected time interval on the dial and was controlled by the setting knob. An interval hand indicated the number of seconds of the interval remaining before the camera would be tripped. The setting knob provided the means of setting the desired time interval.

The recycle knob provided a means of tripping the camera before completion of the preset interval.

The extra picture switch button was located immediately below the interval dial and could be used at any time to take pictures.

An electro-magnetic counter indicated the number of film exposures that had been made.

The aircraft's photographic equipment was installed in the fuselage aft of the pilot's rear bulkhead and was operated from the cockpit. The aft fuselage contained the camera mount, camera mount supports, sway braces, vacuum system, oblique sliding door (port side only), vertical sliding door and door actuating cables.

The following cameras could be fitted in the aft fuselage:

K17-6"	Vertical
K17-12"	Vertical
K17-24"	Vertical
K17-24"	Oblique set at 3°
K17-24"	Oblique set at 15°
k18-24"	Vertical

Below, oblique camera port with door open. The fairing was an oil shield.

49

Previous page top, camera controls mounted to the left-hand side of the cockpit. Previous page bottom, F8F-2P right-hand console comunication controls typical of the F8F-2/-2N/-2P aircraft. Above, side fuselage oblique camera port with shutter door closed. Pilot's step is just below port and large belly access door is open. Below left, empty aft fuselage camera bay just aft of the radio equipment. Below right, K17-6" camera installed in the belly camera port. (National Archives)

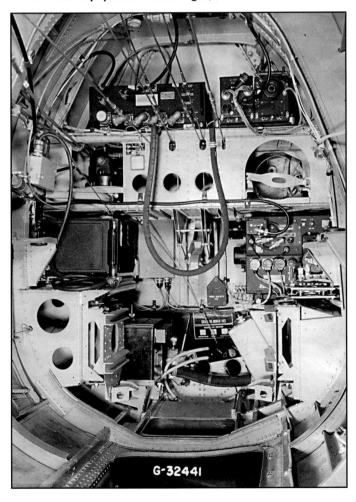

G-32444

G-32440

G-32442

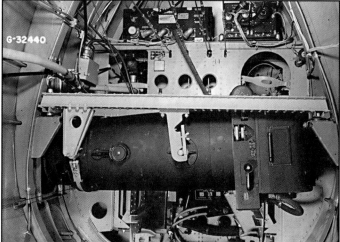

G-32439

52

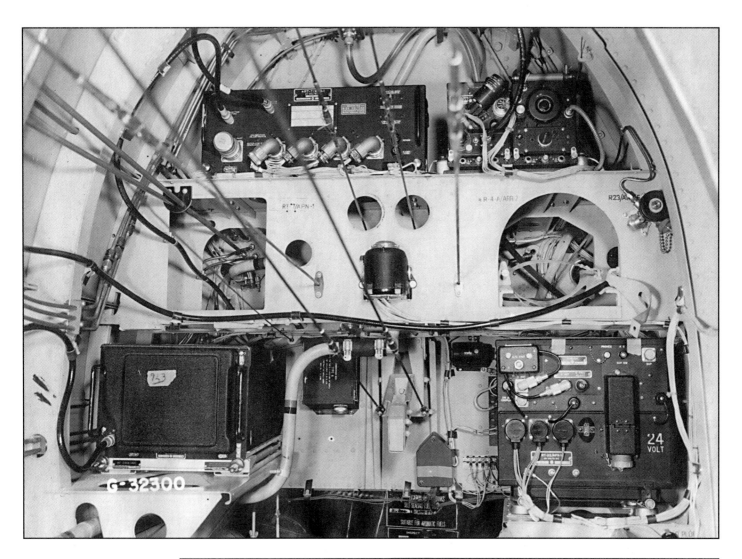

Above, view of F8F-2/2N/2P radio shelves from the rear looking forward. The large cutout in the center right of the photo was the oxygen bottle compartment. At right, oxygen bottle installation as seen from below. The bottle was located on the lower right side aft of the pilot's aft bulkhead. See page 45. Previous page illustrates alternate camera installations on the F8F-2P. At top left, K17-12" vertical camera installation. At top right, K17-24" vertical camera installation. At lower left, K18-24" vertical camera installation. At middle right, K17-24" oblique installation set at 3°. Bottom right, K17-24" oblique installation set at 15°. (all photos National Archives)

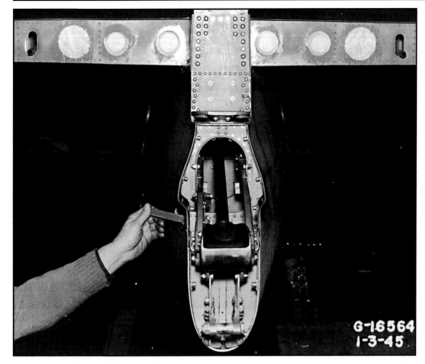

G-16564
1-3-45.

Above, stowed tailhook with tail cone removed viewed from behind. At right, tailhook extended in the landing configuration. (Grumman)

1. Hook Assembly—#57202
2. Aft Track Assembly—#57210 (IL & 1R)
3. Down-Lock Switch Installation—#56523
4. Forward Track Assembly—#57214
5. Carriage Assembly—#57201
6. Up-Lock Bolt—#58939
7. Control Cable Assembly—#56952
8. Pulley Bracket Installation—#56938
9. Lowering Control Installation—#57223
10. Chain Guide Tube Assembly—#57625
11. Operating Chain Assembly—#57213
12. Down Lock Release Mechanism

13. Operating Cable Pulley Assembly
   Pulley—AN210-4A
   Bolt—AN4-12A
   Washer—G169-416(2)
   Nut—AN365-428
14. Guide Roller Assembly
   Roller—#58936
   Bolt—AN4-22A
   Washer—G169-416T
   Nut—AN365-428
15. Cockpit Control Handle—#56892
16. Control Guard Assembly—#56882
17. Control Cable Pulley—AN210-3
18. Pulley Support Block—#58876
19. Position Indicator Light

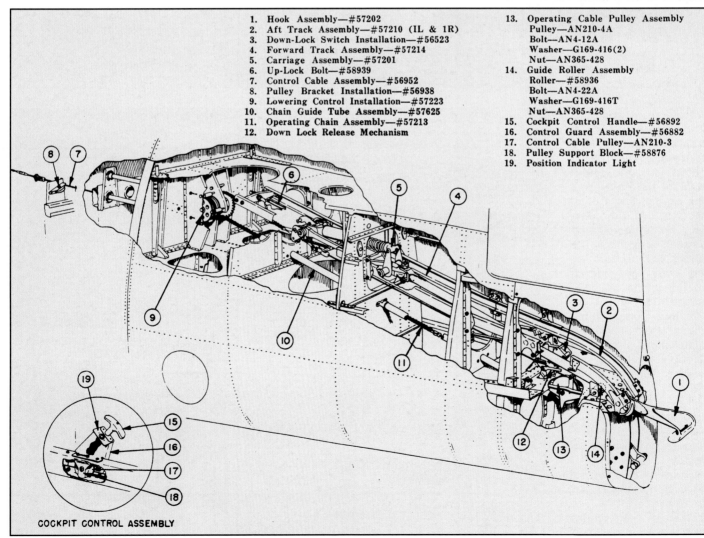

COCKPIT CONTROL ASSEMBLY

Above, head-on view of folded wings on the XF8F-1. (USN) At right, right wing fold. (Ginter) Below and bottom, left wing fold. Note Pitot tube location. (National Archives)

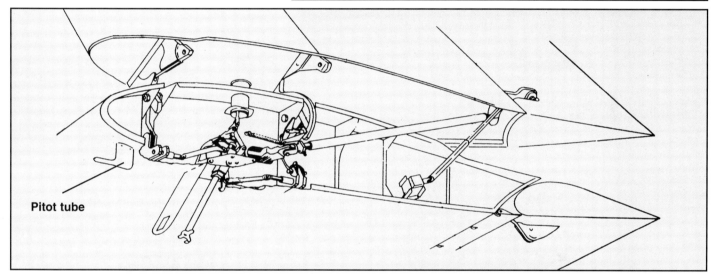

Pitot tube

F8F LANDING GEAR AND TAILHOOK CONTROLS

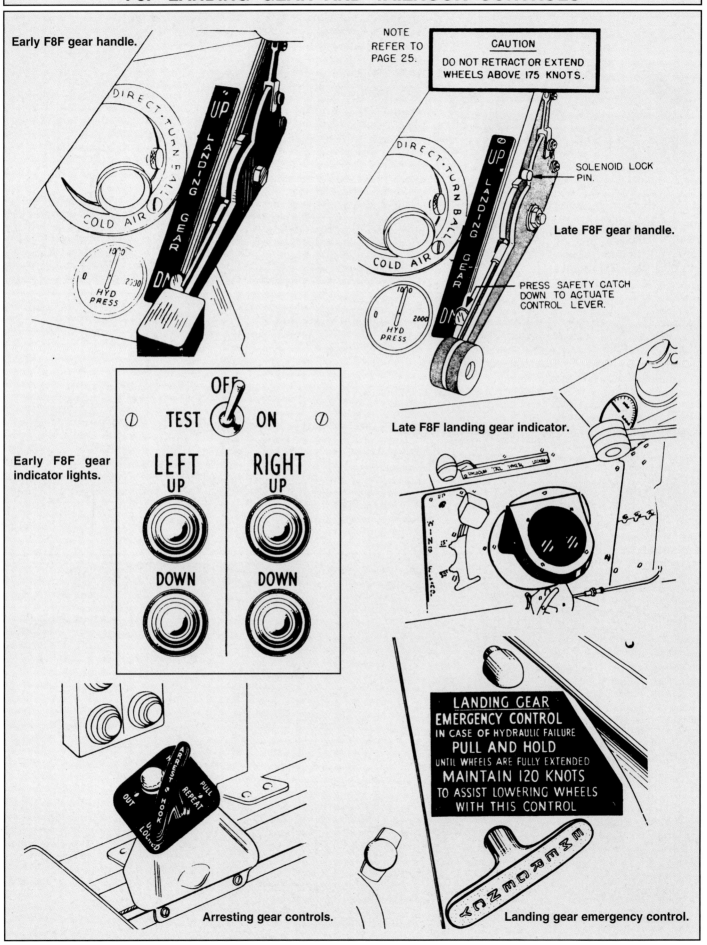

Early F8F gear handle.

NOTE
REFER TO
PAGE 25.

CAUTION
DO NOT RETRACT OR EXTEND
WHEELS ABOVE 175 KNOTS.

SOLENOID LOCK PIN.

Late F8F gear handle.

PRESS SAFETY CATCH DOWN TO ACTUATE CONTROL LEVER.

OFF
TEST   ON

Early F8F gear indicator lights.

LEFT
UP

RIGHT
UP

DOWN

DOWN

Late F8F landing gear indicator.

LANDING GEAR
EMERGENCY CONTROL
IN CASE OF HYDRAULIC FAILURE
PULL AND HOLD
UNTIL WHEELS ARE FULLY EXTENDED
MAINTAIN 120 KNOTS
TO ASSIST LOWERING WHEELS
WITH THIS CONTROL

Arresting gear controls.

Landing gear emergency control.

G-16164
8-24-44

Above, F8F-2 tail wheel swiveled 180°. (Ginter) At right and below, XF8F-1 tail wheel. (National Archives)

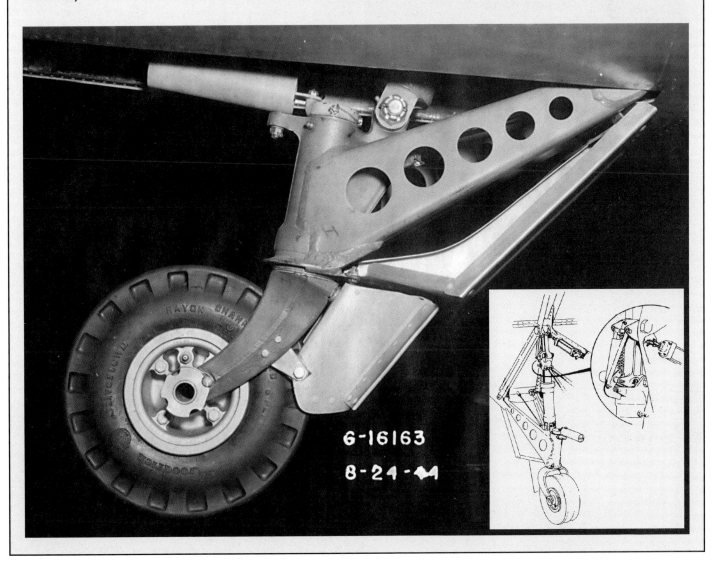

6-16163
8-24-44

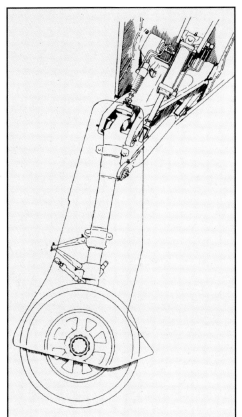

Above and below, main gear outer door layout and location. At right, upper gear hinges and mounting geometry. (National Archives)

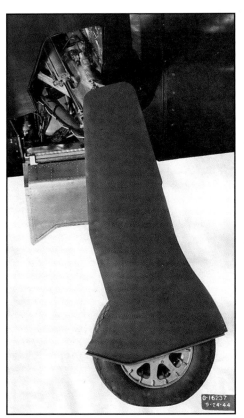

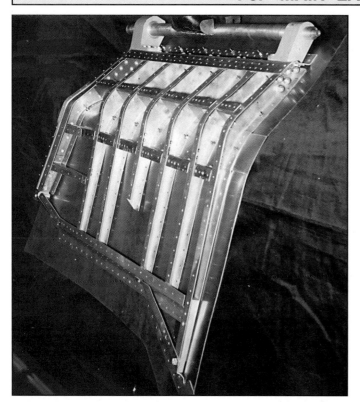

Above left, XF8F-1 inner main gear door prior to having its skin applied. (National Archives) Above right, the inner main gear door on an F8F-2 aircraft. (Ginter) Below, F8F-2 right main gear well looking aft. (Ginter)

Above and below, landing gear retraction tests conducted on 13 March 1945. Note open aft fuselage access door. (MFR)

G-16112

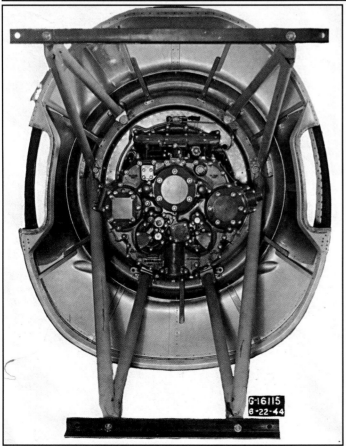

G-16115
6-22-44

G-32294

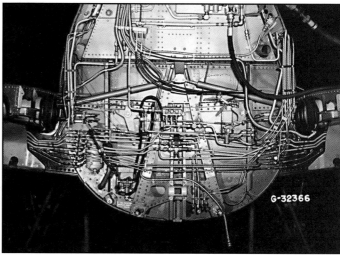

Above, engine firewall upper section. Above right, engine firewall lower portion. Below left, right side view of the engine accessory section. Below right, left side view of the engine accessory section. Bottom left, right side view of the lower engine accessory section viewed through the gear well. Bottom right, left side view of the lower engine accessory section viewed through the gear well. (all photos National Archives) Previous page top, R-2800-22W engine. Bottom left, rear view of engine quick-change unit with cowlings and engine mount fitted. Bottom right, rear view of completely plumbed engine accessory section. White tank on the right was for water injection. (all photos National Archives)

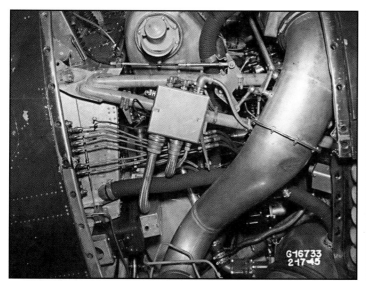

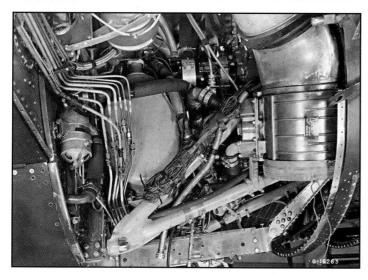

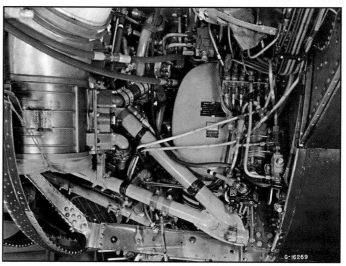

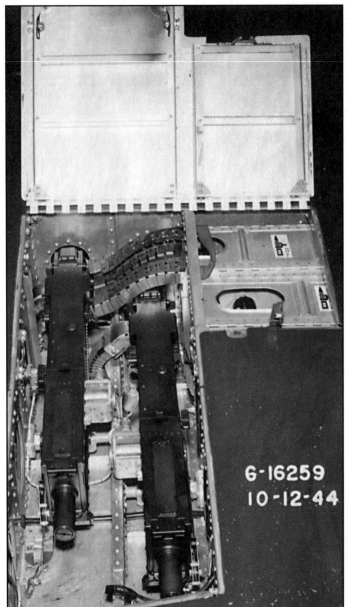

The F8F-1 and F8F-1N were equipped with four .50 cal machine guns. Each outboard gun had 200 rounds and each inboard gun had 325 rounds. The guns were charged hydraulically and fired electrically by a switch on the control stick. The gun charger control handles, one for the left and one for the right wing guns, was located at the base of the main instrument panel.

At left, F8F-1 right wing gunbay showing twin .50 calibre machine guns with their ammo boxes to the right. Above, F8F-1B .50 calibre gunports. Gun camera was located in the leading edge opening at left. Bottom left, pitot tube was located under the left wing. Landing light is also seen here. Below, NAS Anacostia reserve F8F-1 being rearmed. .50 calibre ammo is being loaded into one of the aircraft's ammo boxes. (all photos National Archives)

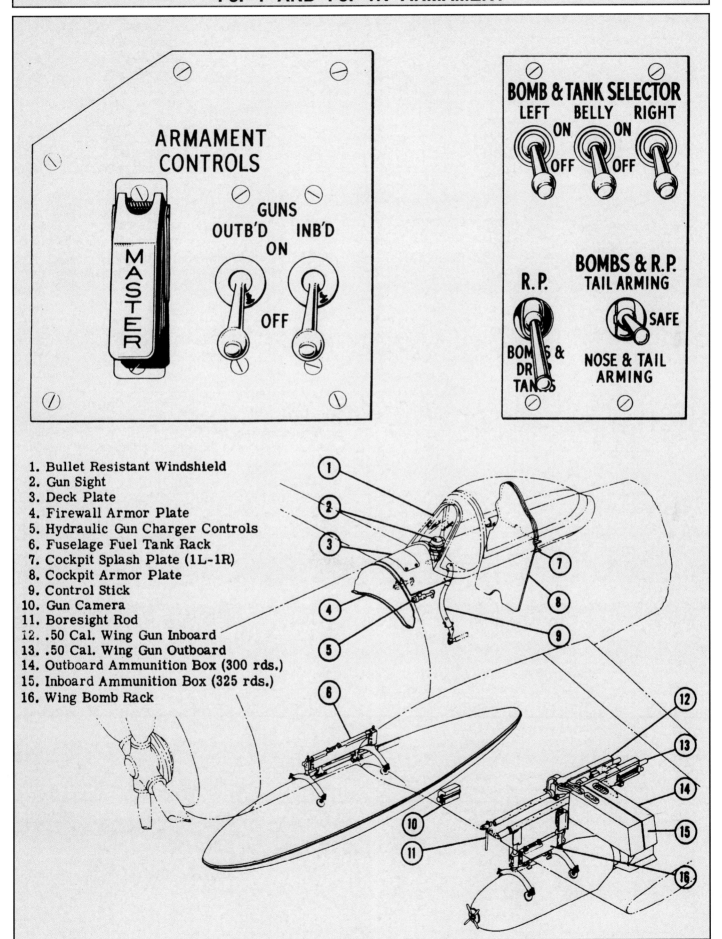

ARMAMENT CONTROLS

MASTER

GUNS

OUTB'D   INB'D

ON

OFF

BOMB & TANK SELECTOR

LEFT   BELLY   RIGHT

ON   ON

OFF   OFF

R.P.

BOMBS & DR. TANKS

BOMBS & R.P.
TAIL ARMING

SAFE

NOSE & TAIL
ARMING

1. Bullet Resistant Windshield
2. Gun Sight
3. Deck Plate
4. Firewall Armor Plate
5. Hydraulic Gun Charger Controls
6. Fuselage Fuel Tank Rack
7. Cockpit Splash Plate (1L-1R)
8. Cockpit Armor Plate
9. Control Stick
10. Gun Camera
11. Boresight Rod
12. .50 Cal. Wing Gun Inboard
13. .50 Cal. Wing Gun Outboard
14. Outboard Ammunition Box (300 rds.)
15. Inboard Ammunition Box (325 rds.)
16. Wing Bomb Rack

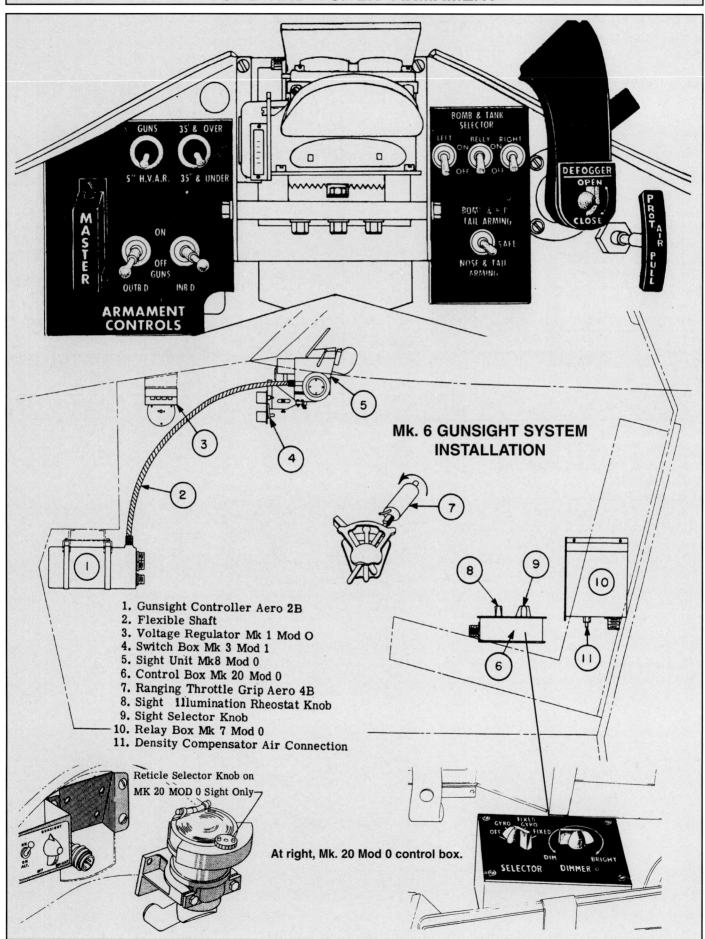

GUNS 35° & OVER

5" H.V.A.R. 35° & UNDER

MASTER

ON
OFF
GUNS
OUTB'D INB'D

ARMAMENT
CONTROLS

BOMB & TANK
SELECTOR

LEFT BELLY RIGHT
ON ON
OFF OFF

BOMB & P.F
TAIL ARMING

SAFE

NOSE & TAIL
ARMING

DEFOGGER
OPEN

CLOSE

PROT
AIR
PULL

Mk. 6 GUNSIGHT SYSTEM
INSTALLATION

1. Gunsight Controller Aero 2B
2. Flexible Shaft
3. Voltage Regulator Mk 1 Mod O
4. Switch Box Mk 3 Mod 1
5. Sight Unit Mk8 Mod 0
6. Control Box Mk 20 Mod 0
7. Ranging Throttle Grip Aero 4B
8. Sight Illumination Rheostat Knob
9. Sight Selector Knob
10. Relay Box Mk 7 Mod 0
11. Density Compensator Air Connection

Reticle Selector Knob on
MK 20 MOD 0 Sight Only

GUNSIGHT
ON
ON
ALT.
OFF

At right, Mk. 20 Mod 0 control box.

FIXED
GYRO GYRO
OFF FIXED

DIM BRIGHT

SELECTOR DIMMER

F8F-1B, F8F-2 AND F8F-2N ARMAMENT

The F8F-1B, F8F-2 and F8F-2N aircraft were equipped with four 20mm cannons and the F8F-2P was equipped with two 20mm cannons on the inboard station only. All cannons were fitted with flash shields. Each inboard gun had 225 rounds and each outer gun had 188 rounds. Layout of the gun bays and ammo box compartments was the same as those shown for the .50 calibre machine guns seen on page 64. The guns were charged hydraulically and fired electrically by a switch on the control stick. The gun charger control handles, one for the left and one for the right wing guns, was located at the base of the main instrument panel.

At right, Marine reservists loading 20mm ammo belts into a NAS Denver-based F8F-2 in 1951. (USN)

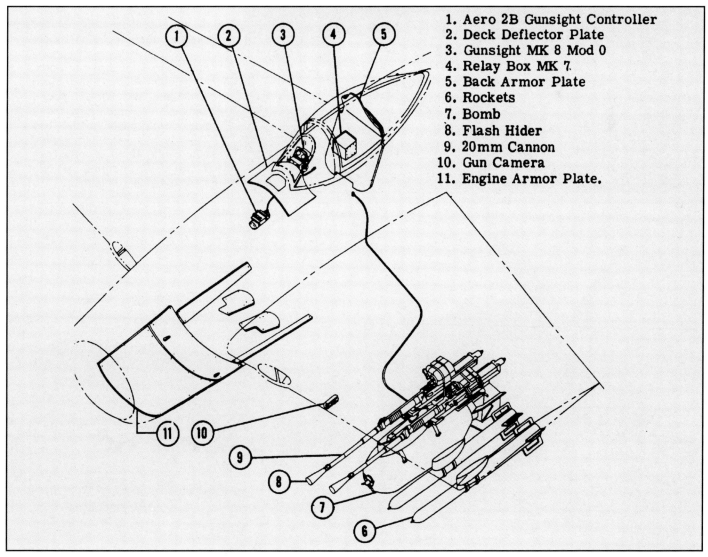

1. Aero 2B Gunsight Controller
2. Deck Deflector Plate
3. Gunsight MK 8 Mod 0
4. Relay Box MK 7
5. Back Armor Plate
6. Rockets
7. Bomb
8. Flash Hider
9. 20mm Cannon
10. Gun Camera
11. Engine Armor Plate.

WING STORES

Above and at left, the number two production F8F-1 BuNo 90438 fitted with two Douglas-built twin .50 calibre gun pods. (Grumman) Below, F8F-1 BuNo 90438 fitted with two 500 pound bombs. Alternate wing loads were: two 1,000lb bombs, two 250lb bombs, six 100lb bombs, two 650lb depth bombs, two 325lb depth bombs, or two 1,000lb mines. (Grumman)

WING STORES

Above and at right, F8F-1 BuNo 90438 seen testing two 1,150lb, 11.75 inch, Tiny Tim air launched rockets. Initially, they were tested with a six-foot firing lanyard, but when fired the Bearcat would disappear in a cloud of smoke. A twelve-foot lanyard finally solved the problem. (Grumman) Below, four 5" rockets mounted on F8F-1 BuNo 94759 while assigned as a test ship at NAF Naval Ordnance Test Station (NOTS) Inyokern, CA. In addition to the standard wing pylon, the Bearcat had four Mk. 9 rocket pylons for use with 5" HVAR rockets. This Bearcat has been retrofitted with the rollover structure. (William Swisher)

WING TANKS

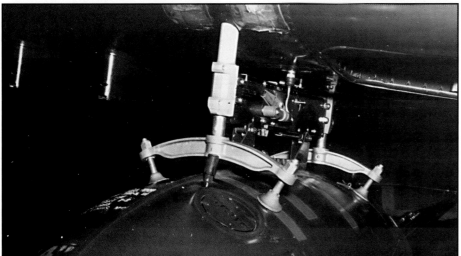

Above, F8F-1 BuNo 90443 with two 300 gallon ferry drop tanks installed. These tanks increased the Bearcat's radius of action for ferry missions by almost three times but lowered the cruise speed by 45 mph. Two full 300 gallon tanks had the same weight as two 2,000lb bombs. These tanks were not used at sea. (Grumman) At left, sway brace details on a 100 gallon wing drop tank. (Grumman) Bottom, F8F-1 BuNo 90438 with two Mk. 4 100 gallon wing drop tanks and a centerline Mk. 5 150 gallon fuel tank. (Grumman)

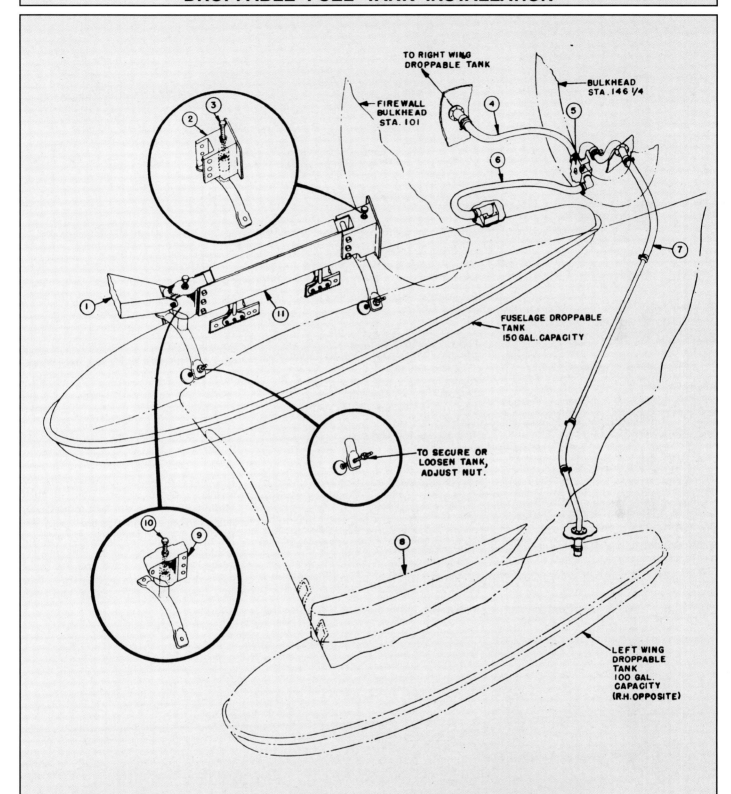

TO RIGHT WING
DROPPABLE TANK

FIREWALL
BULKHEAD
STA. 101

BULKHEAD
STA. 146 1/4

FUSELAGE DROPPABLE
TANK
150 GAL. CAPACITY

TO SECURE OR
LOOSEN TANK,
ADJUST NUT.

LEFT WING
DROPPABLE
TANK
100 GAL.
CAPACITY
(R.H. OPPOSITE)

1. Droppable Tank Rack Beam Assembly—#55114
2. Droppable Tank Rack Rear Fitting—#58363
3. Sway Brace Adjustment
    Bolt—#58361
    Nut—AN366-F624
4. Right Wing Droppable Tank Feed Line Assembly
5. Tank Selector Valve Assembly—#55369

6. Belly Droppable Tank Feed Line Assembly—#55399
7. Left Wing Droppable Tank Feed Line Assembly
8. Wing Bomb Rack Assembly #53512
9. Droppable Tank Rack Forward Fitting—#58362
10. Sway Brace Adjustment
    Bolt—#58361   Nut—AN316-6R
11. Mk. 51 Model 7G Bomb Rack—#B. O. 328759

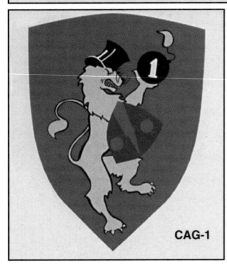

CAG-1

On 1 September 1948, the Chief of Naval Operations ordered the CAG units to be designated as Composite Squadrons (VC).

Bearcat Air Groups: CAG-1 "T" became VC-10, CAG-3 "K" became VC-30, CAG-5 "S" became VC-50, CAG-6 "C" became VC-60, CAG-7 "L" became VC-70, CAG-9 "PS" became VC-90, CAG-11 "V" became VC-110, CAG-13 "P" became VC-130, CAG-15 "A" became VC-150, CAG-17 "R" became VC-170, and CAG-19 "B" became VC-190. The VC assigned aircraft were numbered with two numerals starting with 00.

The VC units were comprised of the CAG and a host of specialized aircraft teams utilizing a mixed bag of aircraft. An example of their possible makeup is shown below for VC-10's World Cruise deployment aboard the USS Tarawa (CV-40) from 28 September 1948 through 21 February 1949.

F8F-1	CAG
F6F-5N	Night Fighter Team, FAWTUPAC Det 40
F8F-2P (2)	Photo Team, VC-61 Det 40
TBM-3E	ASW Team, VC-21 Det 40
TBM-3W	AEW Team, VC-11 Team 9
TBM-3N	VR Team
TBM-3Q	ECM Team

Administrative control of the VC unit was assigned to one of the Air Group's squadrons, in this case VF-13. The VC units were formed for each deployment then disbanded afterwards. After June 1949 the system of CAG VC squadrons was discontinued in favor of small squadron Dets to accomodate the Air Group's needs for night fighters, photo birds, ASW, AEW, and ECM aircraft.

Prior to the Air Group VC concept, up to four F6F-5Ps were assigned to the Air Groups for their photographic needs. They would be embedded into either the first fighter squadron or into both the first and second fighter squadrons and would carry the respective squadron's modex, either 1XX or 2XX.

Above, CVG-1 CAG CDR Bush Bringle in F8F-1 BuNo 95131 (T/00) at NAS Moffett Field, CA, on 4 October 1948. (NMNA) Below, same aircraft with VF-1B's Commanding Officer warming-up behind the CAG bird. (William T. Larkins) The rudder tab and the tip of the belly tank were painted the four squadron colors red, yellow, blue, and orange.

The primary mission of the Naval Air Test Center (NATC) is to determine an aircraft's suitability for usage in the fleet. During the late '40s and early '50s, NATC project pilots and engineers were divided among five test divisions. Flight Test (FT) concentrated on aircraft and engine performance, stability and control and carrier suitability. Tactical Test (TT) evaluated tactical flying suitability, Service Test (ST) evaluated operational suitability, emphasizing maintenance. Electronic Test (ET) was responsible for all the avionics equipment. Armament Test (AT) evaluated the aircraft as a weapons platform.

Additionally, the NATC supplied

At top, NATC F8F-1 assigned to the System Test Division passes low over the beach. ST47 was painted in yellow. (via Tailhook) Above, Armament Test (AT-18) F8F-1C BuNo 94803 on 28 September 1945. (USN via Fred Roos) Below, Tactical Test (TT-8) F8F-2N. (via Dave Menard)

an evaluation team to the contractor's plant for a Preliminary Evaluation (NPE), a formal series of tests with the prototype models prior to the aircraft's arrival at NATC, and conducted fleet suitability evaluations using the test center's aircraft. Finally, the Service Test Division (ST) aircraft and personnel were later involved in the Fleet Introductory Program (FIP), which trained the first squadron, its pilots, and ground crews scheduled to operate the new aircraft.

Above, XF8F-2 BuNo 95049 at Patuxent River, MD, on 18 July 1949. The factory nose number 049 was wearing away. Below, F8F-2 BuNo 121599 at Pax on 26 May 1949. Bottom, Flight Test (FT) F8F-2 BuNo 121594 at NATC on 31 March 1950. (all National Archives via D. Lucabaugh)

Above and at right, Tactical Test (TT) XF8F-1 BuNo 90447 at Annapolis, MD, on 9 October 1945. (Ben Ederr via Lucabaugh)

NOTS INYOKERN, CALIFORNIA

The Naval Air Facility, China Lake, CA, provided support to the Naval Ordnance Test Station (NOTS), China Lake, for research, development, test and evaluation of guided missiles, aircraft weapons delivery systems, aircraft rockets and rocket launchers, aviation fire control systems, and underwater ordnance.

Below, NOTS Inyokern F8F-1 BuNo 94759 with four 5" rockets mounted on its wings at Edwards AFB in May 1950. (William Swisher) Bottom, NOTS Inyokern F8F-2D BuNo 122690 on 5 November 1954. At least one other F8F-2D, BuNo 121698 which made a wheels-up landing on 18 April 1952, was assigned to NOTS Inyokern. (Dave Ostrowski)

NAVAL AIR MISSILE TEST CENTER, NAMTC
NAS POINT MUGU, CALIFORNIA

The Naval Air Missile Test Center was responsible for the fleet implementation of missile-based weapon systems on naval aircraft.

Besides the two F8F-1s seen below, NAMTC operated at least one F8F-2D drone control aircraft, BuNo 121784.

Below, two NAMTC F8F-1s in flight. The upper aircraft had 159 and POINT MUGU painted under the wing. (NMNA) Bottom, Monterey Post Graduate School had a number of different types of aircraft assigned over the years so that pilots could maintain their proficiency while attending the school. F8F-2 BuNo 122636 seen here on 30 October 1955 was possibly the last Bearcat in active Navy service. (William Swisher)

NAVAL POST GRADUATE SCHOOL MONTEREY, CALIFORNIA

CARRIER AIRCRAFT SERVICE UNITS (CASU)

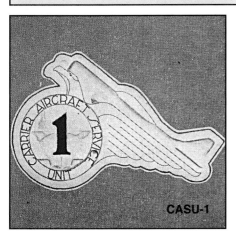

CASU-1

Above right and below, CASU-1 F8F-1 BuNo 95443 in flight near Pearl Harbor on 27 July 1945. Fuselage and wing lettering was white. CASU-1 was stationed at NAS Ford Island, CASU-2 was at NAS Barbers Point, CASU-4 at NAS Puunene, CASU-31 at NAS Hilo, CASU-32 at NAS Kahului, and CASU-38 was assigned to NAS Kaneohe. (USN via NMNA and D. Lucabagh)

Above, Ford Island-based CASU-1 F8F-1. (via Bob Rocker/Tailhook) Below, CASU-5 F8F-1 nosed-over while taxiing at NAS San Diego on 18 January 1946. Fuselage code C57 was in painted in yellow. (USN)

A CASU-25 F8F-1, BuNo 94879, was struck after the pilot stalled it on take-off on 23 May 1946. The injured pilot did survive.

On 11 July 1946, the CASUs were ordered replaced with FASRONs by 1 January 1947.

Above, CASU-6 F8F-1 BuNo 94788 at Haywood, CA, on 14 April 1946. Like CASU-5, the fuselage and wing lettering was yellow. (NMNA) Below, three CASU-5 F8F-1s near San Diego on 12 December 1945. Fuselage lettering was in yellow. BuNo 94824 is in the foreground. (NMNA)

FASRON 11

Above, FASRON-1 F8F-1 BuNo 95491 in March 1949. (NMNA) Below, FASRON-11 F8F-1 BuNo 95491 in flight on 12 November 1948. (NMNA) Bottom, NADC Johnsville-based F8F-1D BuNo 90446. (USN)

From 1 January 1947 through 1960, shore based FASRONS were responsible for the majority of maintenance on Navy aircraft. After 1960, the parent squadron was responsible for all maintenance short of overhaul and the FASRONS were disestablished. At least 13 FASRONS had Bearcats assigned. These were: FASRON-1, 2, 3, 4, 5, 6, 7, 8, 9, 10, 11, 112, and 691.

NAVAL AIR DEVELOPMENT CENTER JOHNSVILLE

VCN-1

On 1 April 1946, Night Air Combat Training Units (NACTU) were redesignated. NACTU (Atlantic) and NACTU (Pacific) became Night Development Squadrons Atlantic

FAWTUPAC

(NACTULant) and Pacific (NACTUPac). On 15 November 1946, the two squadrons became NightDevRons (VCNs). VCN-1 was stationed at NAS Barbers Point, T.H, and VCN-2 was located at NAS Miami and at NAF Key West, FL. VCN-1 and VCN-2 were redesignated Fleet All-Weather Training Units (FAWTUPAC and FAWTULANT) on 1 August 1948.

In late 1946, VCN-1/2 would receive the twelve F7F-4N Tigercats built specially for carrier operations to supplement their fleet of F6F-5Ns, TBM-3Ns and a handfull of F8F-1Ns. The Bearcats were found to be ill suited as night fighters as they were short-legged due to lack of fuel reserves and their performance suffered dramatically when carrying the APS-19 radar pod. The Hellcats

Above, VCN-1 F8F-1N. (USN) Below, VCN-1 F8F-1N BuNo 95320 PA/22 after a Davis barrier crash aboard CV-45 on the night of 15 November 1947, when the left landing gear collapsed and the right wing broke off and the belly tank caught fire. LT F.S. Moody walked away uninjured. (via Corwin Meyer)

therefore continued on as the Fleet's night fighter until replaced by F5U-5N Corsairs.

VCN-1 lost BuNo 95161 and its pilot at Barbers Point when he undershot his landing on 16 October 1947 and hit the trees. Another F8F-1N, BuNo 95320, was striken after a night barrier crash on CV-45 on 15 November 1947. The pilot, LT F.S. Moody, was uninjured.

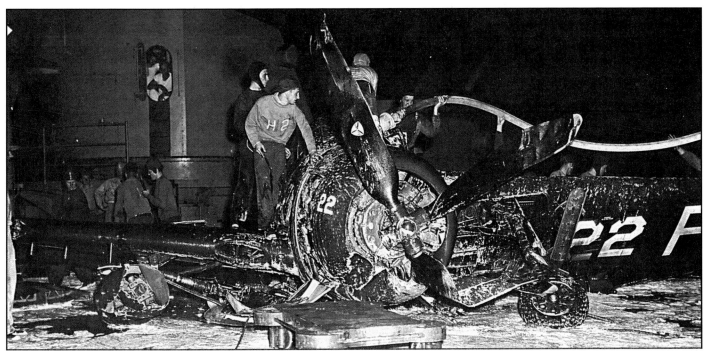

DEVELOPMENT SQUADRON TWO (VX-2), NAAS CHINCOTEAGUE, VA.

NAAS Chincoteague, VA, was established on 5 March 1943 and in January 1946 the Navy established the Naval Air Ordnance Test Station (NAOTS) at "Chinco". The guided missile test facilities and staff were transferred from NAMU Johnsville, PA, to this remote location where missile development could continue in relative secrecy.

Air Development Squadron Two (VX-2) was responsible for in-flight testing and operated numerous F7F-2Ds and F8F aircraft as drone control (for TD2C-1s and F6F-5Ks) and live missile test aircraft. The Bearcats were operated under numerous designations. Known F8Fs assigned to VX-2 were: XF8F-1 BuNo 90444; F8F-1 BuNo 94752; F8F-1B BuNos 95166, 95319; F8F-1D BuNos 90447, 90451, 90452, 90455-90457, 94752, 95009; F8F-2D BuNos 121724-121725

Below, VX-2 ramp at Chincotegue, VA, in December 1949. Six F7F-2Ds can be seen along with two TBMs, eight F8Fs, one JRB, ten JDs, twelve Culvers, two PBYs, one PB4Y-2 and eleven F6F-5K drones. (USN via B.J. Long) Bottom, five VX-2 Bearcats with F8F-2D BuNo 121725 (XB/03) in the foreground in 1949. 121725 was in standard drone control colors of engine blue/grey with orange-yellow wings and tail trimmed in insignia red. The next three aircraft (probably F8F-1Bs) were glossy sea blue with white markings. (Roger Besecker)

Above, two VX-2 F8F-2D drone control aircraft escort a Hellcat drone. (via Norm Taylor) Middle, NAOTS TD2C-1 target drone being controlled by a VX-2 Bearcat target control aircraft on 29 December 1949. (USN via B. J. Long) Below, VX-2 F8F-2D BuNo 121724 at NAS Norfolk, VA, in June 1951 with a red F6F-5K drone next to it. (NMNA)

Above, two VX-2 F8F-1D Bearcat drone control aircraft, BuNos 90447 and 90456, near NAOTS Chincoteague, VA, on 29 December 1949. (USN via B. J. Long) Below, VX-2 F8F-2D on display at NAAS Chincoteague in 1952. (Roger F. Besecker)

UTILITY SQUADRON TWO (VU-2), NAS OCEANA, VA

Utility Squadron Two (VU-2) was initially a detachment of Utility Squadron Four (VU-4) at NAS Quonset Point, RI. As the demand for utility services increased, the VU-4 Det was established on 8 January 1952. The squadron was originally equipped with the F8F-2 Bearcat, JD-1 (A-26) Invader and the F9F Panther. The F9F Cougar followed shortly thereafter. FJ-3 Furys were also added and the unit moved to NAS Oceana, VA, in June 1960. Detachment Alfa remained at NAS Quonset Point with the JDs. In 1961,

the supersonic F8U-1 Crusader replaced the squadron's Furys.

The squadron provided fleet utility services until redesignated Fleet Composite Squadron Four (VC-4) on 1 July 1965.

Below, at least two F8F-2s, BuNo 121655 coded UJ-41 and BuNo 121584 coded UJ-44, were flown at Utility Squadron Two. (USN)

UTILITY SQUADRON THREE (VU-3/VU-3K)

WWII Utility Squadron VJ-3 was redesignated VU-3 in July 1946. The squadron was disestablished in late 1947 and reestablished as VU-3 in December 1948. Flying from MAF Santa Ana, MCAS El Toro, NAS Miramar and NAF Ream Field, CA, VU-3K flew two F7F-2D Tigercats as well as F6F-5D Hellcats and six F8F-1D Bearcats as drone control aircraft for F6F-5K Hellcat drones. In 1951, F8F-2Ds replaced the F8F-1Ds with

the squadron maintaining eight Bearcats until they were withdrawn from service in July 1954. The squadron's tail code was "UF".

VU-4 was originally established as VJ-4 on 15 November 1940 at NAS Norfolk, VA. During the war, VJ-4 operated PBY Catalinas on anti-submarine patrol and on rescue missions. After WWII, on 15 November 1946, the squadron became Utility Squadron Four and was stationed at NAF Chincoteague, VA. The unit was responsible for fleet support in air-to-air and surface-to-air weapons training. The squadron operated Bearcats and Tigercats through June 1954. VU-4 was redesignated VC-4 on 1 July 1965.

Above right, two views of VU-4 F8F-2D BuNo 121704 (UD/61) in 1953-54. (Dave Lucabaugh, Brian Baker) At right, VU-4 F8F-2Ds BuNos 122663 (UD/60) and 121704 (UD/61) run-up next to two Hellcat drones. (Balogh via Menard) Below, VU-4 F8F-2D BuNo 122663. (NMNA)

UTILITY SQUADRON FIVE (VU-5), NAS QUONSET POINT, R.I.

VU-5 was established on 16 August 1950 in order to provide utility services to the fleet in and around the islands of Japan. The unit's primary mission was to provide targets for both the aerial and surface components of the fleet. They also provided photo services, adversary services and airborne control of surface launched missiles. VU-5 became VC-5 on 1 July 1965.

Utility Squadron Five operated at least four Bearcats in 1948-1949. These were BuNos 90438, 90439,

90447, and 90457. All wore the XF8F-1 designation on the aft fuselage.

Below, colorful XF8F-1 BuNo 90439 at NAS Quonset Point, RI, in 1949. This Bearcat and the Avengers in the background were painted dark engine blue/grey with yellow wings and tail surfaces. The rudder was red/orange and the wings had a large red/orange stripe. The thin white line on the fuselage side runs between two foot and hand holds used to access the wing and cockpit. (Billy Jack Long)

UTILITY SQUADRON SEVEN (VU-7)

Utility Squadron Seven (VU-7) was established on 4 December 1942 at NAS Alameda, CA, with the mission of providing utility aircraft services to units of the Pacific Fleet. These services included the towing of aerial targets and launching drone targets for surface-to-air and air-to-air

gunnery and missile firing. VU-7 relocated to NAAS Miramar, CA, from April 1949 through September 1951. VU-7 was redesignated Fleet Composite Squadron Seven (VC-7)

on 1 July 1965.

Above, VU-7 F8F-2 BuNu 121765 at NAAS Miramar. (USN)

U.S.S. SAIPAN

VX-3

5Ns. In November 1946, VF-1L was equipped with eleven F8F-1s, eleven F6F-5s, four F6F-5Ns, and ten F4U-4s. In August 1948, the squadron's complement was sixteen F8F-1s, nine F4U-4s, four F6F-5Ns, five FH-1 Phantom jets and one SNJ.

VF-1L was established as VF-58 on 15 march 1946 and received F8F-1 Bearcats and was redesignated VF-1L on 15 November 1946. The squadron, along with its parent association CVLG-1, was disestablished on 20 November 1948.

VF-1L was very much like the WWII and post-WWII VC squadrons in that it was made up of many different aircraft to satisfy all the intended VF missions on a CVL. As such, it shared the USS Saipan (CVL-48) with VA-1L equipped with a mixed bag of TBMs, SB2Cs and even F6F-

The unit deployed twice aboard the Saipan. The first deployment was a shakedown cruise to the Caribbean from 3 April through 25 May 1947. The second cruise was from 7 February through 24 February 1948 to Venezuela. While off Venezuela in February, the squadron participated in a fly-over during the inauguration ceremonies in Caracas for President-elect Romulo Gallegos.

During the first cruise, F8F-1 BuNo 95372 was lost when it was safely ditched during approach on 18 May 1947. Between cruises, one aircraft, BuNo 95199, was damaged at NAS Atlantic City, NJ, when the landing gear collapsed on landing on 11 December 1947.

VF-1L's and VA-1A's aircraft and other assets were transferred to VX-3

on 20 November 1948 when the new unit became responsible for Saipan's airwing. A VX-3 F8F-1, BuNo 95122, was severly damaged and its pilot was injured during a barrier landing on the USS Saipan on 30 November 1948. Another VX-3 Bearcat, F8F-2N BuNo 121603, was successfully ditched off the beach at Haven, NJ, on 25 April 1949.

Below, VF-1L F8F-1 BuNo 94786 with squadron's insignia on the engine cowl taxiing in 1947. (NMNA)

FIGHTER SQUADRON VF-1A/VF-11 "RED RIPPERS"

VF-11 was established on 1 February 1927 as VF-5 at Hampton Roads, VA. The squadron started flying Curtiss F6C-3s then transitioned to Boeing F3B-1s, Boeing F4B-1s, Grumman FF-1s, F3F-1s and were flying F4F-3s when WWII broke out. VF-5 became VB-5S (7-1-27), VF-5B (1-1-28), VB-1B (7-1-28), VF-5B (7-1-30), VF-5S (7-1-32), VF-5B (4-1-33),

VF-4 (7-1-37), VF-41 (3-15-41), and then VF-4 (8-4-43). After the war, with F6F Hellcats, they became VF-1A on 15 November 1946. In 1947, they acquired the F8F-1 Bearcat and on 2 August 1948, the squadron was redesignated VF-11.

While designated VF-1A a number of Bearcat mishaps occurred. A pilot was injured and his aircraft, BuNo 95057, was lost on 4 September 1947 when he spun-in after wave-off from the Tarawa. A second Bearcat, BuNo 95324, hit the barrier on CV-40 the same day. F8F-1 BuNo 94924 was lost on 22 September 1947 when it hit the barrier and continued over the side of the USS Boxer (CV-21). The pilot was recovered uninjured. At NAAS El Centro, CA, on 28 April 1948, BuNo 95001 ground looped injuring the pilot. A pilot and aircraft (BuNo 94771) were lost on 18 July 1948 when they failed to return from a

Combat Air Patrol (CAP) off the USS Tarawa (CV-40). A second pilot and aircraft (BuNo 95047) were lost the same day when it crashed off CV-40 due to bad weather.

VF-11 deployed aboard the Tarawa during its world cruise from 23 September 1948 through 22 February 1949.

On 12 September 1949, Air Group One, with VF-11, VF-12 and VF-13 all flying F8F-1 Bearcats, boarded the USS Philippine Sea (CV-47) for her Caribbean shakedown cruise. Shortly thereafter, the squadron's first aircraft was lost when CAG "Bush" Bringle spun into the

Below, Seven VF-1A F8F-1s in flight near Cecil Field on 26 June 1947. (NMNA)

water after leaving the Dog pattern when a fouled deck was cleared. On 21 November during a early morning launch the squadron lost its second aircraft of the cruise. ENS Vic Menefee took the first launch which was a cold cat shot in F8F-1 BuNo 94760 and flew straight into the sea. He was retrieved unharmed. A third aircraft was struck on 18 October when ENS George Dzamka ended up inverted in the barrier. F8F-1 BuNo 95131 was damaged in a hard landing on 19 November. A wing buckled

on F8F-1 BuNo 95077 after a hard landing on CV-47 on 21 November. The squadron returned to Cecil Field on 22 November 1949.

During carrier qualifications conducted on the USS F.D. Roosevelt (CVB-42) on 9 February 1950, F8F-1 BuNo 95101 crashed into the barrier after a hard landing.

On 14 February 1950, VF-11 departed Cecil for Quonset Point and a short cruise aboard CV-47. The

Philippine Sea joined with the Coral Sea (CVB-43) and the Leyte (CV-32) for North Atlantic Operation Portrex which concluded in March. Due to extreme weather on 28 February, VF-11 crashed three aircraft. ENS Gilbert Wilkes took the barrier in BuNo 94881 (T/113) and sustained heavy damage

---

Below, VF-1A F8F-1s on 26 June 1947. Fin tips were red. (NMNA)

Above, VF-1A F8F-1 BuNo 95001 on 22 June 1947. (William T. Larkins via NMNA) Below, VF-1A F8F-1 BuNo 95324 making a landing attempt aboard CV-40 on 4 September 1947, which ended in floating over the barrier and shearing off two sister ships' (T/101 and T/106) right outer wings before stopping. (NMNA)

including loss of part of the left wing. A second barrier engagement was made by ENS Carl Lee, who ended up on his back when the aircraft (BuNo 95164 T/116) flipped over. The third crash of the day took place when LTJG Tom Cross bounced over the barrier and destroyed his aircraft, as well as the CAG bird and a VF-12 Bearcat (T/208). Also damaged was an AD-4 and an AD-3Q. Another F8F-1, BuNo 94989, crashed on landing and skidded down the deck on 10 March. On 16 March, the Air Group commenced Operation Caribex flying numerous missions against the Vieques Island firing range. On CV-47's return to Quonset Point, VF-11 flew ashore to a new duty base at NAS Jacksonville, FL, on 23 March 1950.

In May 1950, the squadron transitioned to the F2H-1 Banshee for a short period of time before receiving F2H-2s.

Below, VF-1A F8F-1 BuNo 95057 loops around the island on the USS Tarawa (CV-40) on 4 September 1947 before crashing into the sea. (USN)

Above, VF-11 F8F-1 BuNo 94962 bounces on the USS Tarawa (CV-40) on 28 October 1948. (NMNA) Below, ENS G. Wilkes crashed on landing F8F-1 BuNo 94881 on 28 February 1950 aboard the USS Philippine Sea (CV-47). (NMNA)

Above, VF-11 F8F-1 BuNo 94907 crashed on landing aboard (CV-47) on 18 October 1949. The pilot was ENS G. Dzamka. (NMNA)
Below, ENS G. Wilkes crashed on landing F8F-1 BuNo 94881 on 28 February 1950 aboard CV-47. (NMNA)

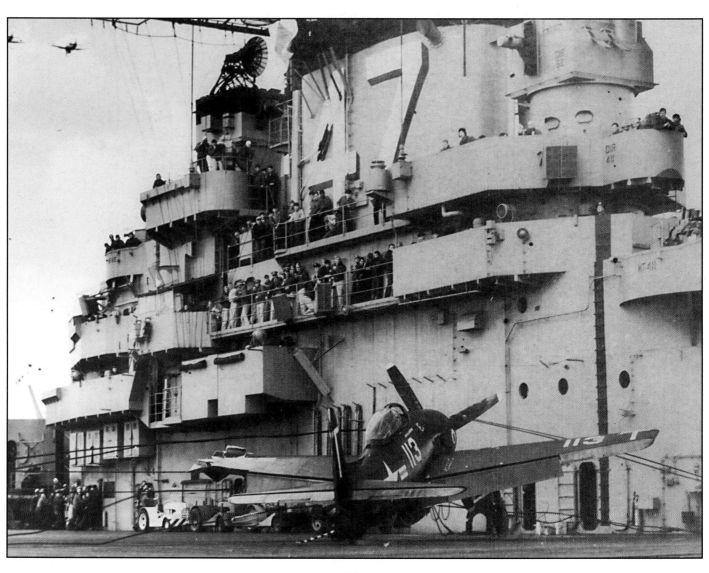

Above, LTJG Wes Rund lands hard aboard the USS Leyte (CV-32) in F8F-1 BuNo 95106 on 3 March 1950. (NMNA) Below, VF-11 F8F-1 BuNo 94907 crashed on landing aboard (CV-47) on 18 October 1949. The pilot was ENS G. Dzamka. (NMNA)

At top, VF-11 night landing accident at NAAS Cecil Field, FL, on 26 July 1949 in F8F-1 BuNo 94929. (NMNA) Above, VF-11 F8F-1 BuNo 95100 after sawing off the tail of BuNo 95119 on 3 May 1950. (NMNA) Below, VF-11 F8F-1 BuNo 95100 at NAS Jacksonville, FL, on 3 May 1950. (NMNA)

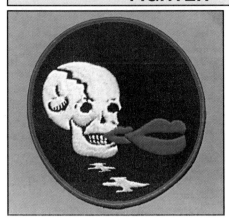

Above, VF-12's LTJG Sherman E. Brent qualified for three Navy "E"s in 1950. Flying an F8F-1, he scored his first "E" for gunnery in February and his second and third "E" for bombing and rocketry in May. (USN) Below, VF-12 F8F-1s T/205 and T/206 on the USS Tarawa (CV-40) on 21 January 1949. (USN)

Established on 12 May 1945 as Fighting Bombing Squadron Four (VBF-4) at NAS Alameda, CA, the "Flying Ubangis" first aircraft was the F4U-4 Corsair. On 15 November 1946, VBF-4 was redesignated Fighter Squadron Two A (VF-2A). In May 1947, the unit started converting to F8F-1 Bearcats and acquired two F6F-5P Hellcats. VF-2A was redesignated Fighter Squadron 12 (VF-12) on 2 August 1948. In September 1950, the squadron started to re-equip with the McDonnell F2H-1 Banshee.

The squadron's Bearcats were involved in three mishaps during 1947. The first took place on 20 August when F8F-1B BuNo 95416 was ditched during a navigation flight near San Diego, injuring the pilot. A minor incident occurred on 2 September when F8F-1B BuNo 95396 hit the catwalk on landing. Another pilot was injured when BuNo 95430 spun-in on landing on CV-40 on 15 September.

During workups for the squadron's first Bearcat cruise, two F8F-1Bs, BuNos 95363 and 95411, were involved in a midair on 15 July 1948. The pilot of 95363 bailed out safely but the pilot of 95411 died in the crash. Another two VF-2A F8F-1Bs, BuNos 95383 and 95425, and their pilots were lost in a midair near the Tarawa on 18 July 1948. VF-12 deployed aboard the USS Tarawa (CV-40) from 1 October 1948 through 21 February 1949 during its World Cruise.

As VF-12, eight more aircraft mishaps occurred with the Bearcat.

While training aboard the USS Midway (CVB-41), F8F-1 BuNo 95371 was damaged when it took the barrier on 31 August 1949. F8F-1 BuNo 95125 was damaged when it was stalled on landing on the USS Philippine Sea (CV-47) on 29 September 1949. A hard landing

damaged F8F-1 BuNo 95063 aboard CV-47 on 29 October 1949. A ground loop at McCalla Field, Cuba, damaged F8F-1 BuNo 94947 on 30 October 1949. Minor damage was done to F8F-1B BuNo 95028 when it swerved off the runway at NAAS Cecil Field, FL, on 2 February 1950. Another F8F-1B, BuNo 122119, hit the barrier on CV-47 on 24 February 1950 when it lost its hook point on landing. A third F8F-1B, BuNo 95285, crash-landed 4 miles NE of Maxwell AFB, AL, on 17 August 1950.

Above, VF-12 F8F-1B BuNo 95253 near NAS Jacksonville in 1949. (NMNA) Below, VF-11 F8F-1 BuNo 95164 piloted by LTJG T. J. Cross hopped the barricade and destroyed a VF-12 Bearcat aboard the USS Philippine Sea (CV-47) on 28 February 1950. (NMNA)

FIGHTER SQUADRON VF-3/VF-3A/VF-31 "TOMCATTERS"

Fighter Squadron Thirty-One started out life as VF-1B on 1 July 1935 with F4B-4s. Redesignated VF-6 on 1 July 1937, the squadron flew F3Fs and later F4Fs. On 15 July 1943, VF-6 became VF-3 and transi-

tioned to F6F Hellcats. The squadron received its first F8F-1 Bearcat in September and on 15 November 1946, the squadron was redesignated VF-3A at NAAS Oceana, VA. The squadron was assigned to the USS Kearsarge (CV-33) and transferred to NAS Quonset Point, RI. The unit conducted CarQuals aboard the USS Franklin D. Roosevelt (CVB-42) during December and qualified aboard Kearsarge in January 1947. Another short cruise on CV-33 was conducted from 3 March through 16 April 1947.

From 7 June through 15 August 1947, the squadron participated in a Midshipman cruise aboard the USS Randolph (CV-15) to the North Atlantic. During the cruise, F8F-1N BuNo 95140 stalled on landing and hit the deck inverted, killing the pilot

on 30 June. Another F8F-1, BuNo 95078, was ditched successfully off Randolph on 25 July 1947. This was followed by short workups aboard the Kearsarge starting in late August. On 20 October, CDR Ed Bayers was relieved by LCDR Lawrence Geis as squadron CO. In March 1948, LCDR Geis ferried the first F8F-1B from Grumman to the unit.

On 7 June 1948, the squadron deployed to the Mediterranean aboard the Kearsarge for a four month cruise which ended on 7 August. During the cruise, VF-3A was

---

Below, LCDR Ed Bayers, CO of VF-3/VF-3A, in F8F-1 BuNo 95151 in 1946. (NMNA)

"FELIX THE CAT"

Above, VF-3 F8F-1 in 1946. (NMNA) At right, squadron pilots at Grumman on 3 October 1947 before ferrying their new Bearcats back to base. CAG-3 CDR A.T. Decker is the pilot second from the left. (USN) Below, VF-3A F8F-1 BuNo 95100 tangled in wires after landing in the Caribbean aboard the USS Kearsarge (CV-33) on 25 March 1947. The pilot was LT F.J. O'Malley. (NMNA)

redesignated VF-31 on 7 August 1948. Once back in CONUS, VF-31 re-qualified aboard the USS Leyte (CV-32) in October and the Kearsarge in November 1948 and February 1949. Meanwhile, the unit had been selected as the first East Coast squadron to transition to the F9F-2 Panther. The first F9F-2 was acquired on 27 December 1949.

As VF-31, four the following Bearcat incidents occurred: F8F-1B BuNo 121515 was damaged during barrier landing on Kearsarge on 11 November 1948. A second F8F-1B, BuNo 121493, was damaged during a hard landing on CV-33 on 20 November 1948. The pilot of F8F-1B BuNo 121506 was injured when he bailed out over Naragansett Bay, RI, due to an inflight fire on 3 February 1949. On 18 May

Above, VF-3A F8F-1 BuNo 95130 at the Cleveland Airport in September 1947. (Peter M. Bowers via NMNA) Below, VF-3A F8F-1 BuNo 95130 at the Cleveland Airport in September 1947. (Peter M. Bowers via NMNA)

1950, F8F-1B BuNo 95148 crash-landed at Barksdale AFB, LA.

Above, VF-3A Bearcats run-up engines prior to launch during a Midshipmen's cruise on the USS Randolph (CV-15) in June 1947. Below, VF-3A Bearcats are inspected by Midshipmen on the Randolph on 18 June 1947. (National Archives)

FIGHTER SQUADRON VF-31 "TOMCATTERS"

Below, feet wet VF-31 Bearcat from the USS Kearsarge (CV-33) after crashing into the sea in 1949. (NMNA)

VBF-3 was established with F6F-3 Hellcats on 1 February 1945 and was redesignated VF-4A on 15 November 1946 and transitioned to F8F-1 Bearcats. VF-4A was redesignated VF-32 on 7 August 1948.

VF-4A made three deployments with the F8F-1 Bearcat, all aboard the USS Kearsarge (CV-33) as part of CVAG-3. The first cruise was in Atlantic waters from 3 March through 16 April 1947. The second was a Midshipman cruise, also in the Atlantic, from 7 June through 16 August 1947. The third cruise to the Mediterranean was in response to the Berlin Crisis from 7 June through 3 October 1948.

During the first cruise, the squadron lost an aircraft and pilot on 14 March 1947 when F8F-1 BuNo 95099 spun-in while attempting to land aboard CV-33. During preparations for the second cruise, F8F-1 BuNo 95335 took the barrier on CV-33 on 1 June 1947. Another F8F-1, BuNo 95216, was damaged in a hard landing on CV-33 on 16 September 1947. This incident was followed by a fatality in BuNo 95337, which hit the banner during a gunnery run and crashed near NAS Quonset Point, RI, on 21 October 1947.

As VF-32, four F8F-1B incidents were recorded. The first occurred when BuNo 122142 collided with an obstacle while taxiing on 1 July 1948. A hard landing on CV-33 damaged BuNo 121502 on 20 November 1948. Then BuNo 121489 flew into the beach killing the pilot near NAS

Jacksonville, FL, while on instruments on 26 May 1949. Another pilot and aircraft, BuNo 121552, were lost on 31 May 1949 when it stalled during landing at Otis AFB, MA.

In late 1949, the squadron began transition to the Vought F4U-4 and the last Bearcat left VF-32 in January 1950. Ironically, the squadron acquired a couple of F8F-2Ps much like earlier F8F squadron's who maintained two-to-four F6F-5Ps. One of these F8F-2Ps, BuNo 121775, made a forced landing, killing the pilot when it exploded 10 miles southwest of Coalinga, CA, on 19 September 1950.

UNOFFICIAL

Above, famous Black Naval Aviator ENS Jesse L. Brown in flight in VF-32 F8F-2 on 11 November 1949. (via Dave Lucabaugh) Below, VF-32 F8F-1B Buno 121463 overturned on landing at NAAS Charlestown in 1949. Fin tip was white(NMNA)

FIGHTER SQUADRON VF-5A "SCREAMING EAGLES"

The Screaming Eagles started out in 1927 as VF-3S flying the Curtiss F6C-4. The squadron designation was soon changed to VF-3B and the Boeing FB-5 replaced the F6C-4. In 1929, the FB-5 gave way to the Boeing F3B-1, which was traded for the Boeing F4B-4 in 1931. In 1935 the retractable gear Grumman F2F-1 joined the squadron. In 1937 the squadron was redesignated VF-5B and upgraded to the Grumman F3F-3. When war broke out on 7 December 1941, the squadron was equipped with Grumman F4F-3 Wildcats.

VF-5B was disestablished on 7 January 1943, and most of the squadron's assets including person-nel were assigned to the newly-established VF-1. Flying Grumman F6F Hellcats, VF-1 was redesignated VF-5 on 15 July 1943. The squadron finished out the war in Vought F4U Corsairs and was redesignated VF-5A on 15 November 1946 while flying the Grumman F8F-1 Bearcat. The Bearcat was replaced by the North American FJ-1 Fury on 18 November 1947 and VF-5A became the first

Above, VF-5A CO CDR Gordon Firebaugh stands next to his aircraft on the deck of the USS Shangri-La (CV-38) in 1947. (USN via Tom Gates/Tailhook) Below, VF-5A CAG bird near San Diego on 5 September 1947. (SDAM)

Navy fleet squadron to operationally deploy jets at sea.

F8F-1 BuNo 95289 stalled on landing aboard the USS Shangri-La (CV-38) and crashed into the sea injuring its pilot on 3 June 1947.

The Screaming Eagles were once again redesignated on 16 August 1948, and became VF-51. The squadron was disestablished on 16 February 1995.

Above, VF-5A pilots at NAS San Diego on 2 August 1947. (USN via Tailhook) Below, twenty-seven VF-5A Bearcats spotted forward of VF-5B's Corsairs on the USS Hornet (CV-12). (National Archives)

Above, VF-5A F8F-1 BuNo 95261 in March 1948 aboard the USS Boxer (CV-21). (Al Schmidt via NMNA) Below, VF-5A F8F-1 BuNo 95374 on deck of the USS Shangri-La (CV-38) in 1947. (NMNA) Bottom, CAG-11 in flight. (SDAM)

Above, VF-5A's Commanding Officer's F8F-1 near San Diego on 5 September 1947. (NMNA) Below, VF-5A F8F-1 aboard the USS Shangri-La (CV-38) in early 1948. (via Tailhook)

VF-52 was originally established as VBF-5 on 8 May 1945 while flying the F6F Hellcat. The squadron next flew Corsairs and was redesignated VF-6A on 15 November 1946 before transitioning to the F8F-1. The squadron was redesignated VF-52 on 16 August 1948 and disestablished on 23 February 1959.

As part of CVAG-5, VF-6A deployed to the Western Pacific aboard the USS Shangri-La (CV-38) from 31 March through 16 June 1947. The squadron went on to fly F9F Panthers during the Korean War.

Above, VF-6A F8F-1 BuNo 95232 being towed past the elevator on CV-38 in 1947. (NMNA) Below, VF-6A F8F-1 BuNo 95232 taxis on CV-38 in 1947. (NMNA)

FIGHTER SQUADRON VF-11A/VF-111 "SUNDOWNERS"

The Sundowners were established as VF-11 on 10 October 1942 and while flying the F6F-5 Hellcat were redesignated VF-11A on 15 November 1946. As VF-11A, one short deployment from 19 November through 25 November 1946 was conducted in the Hellcat before transitioning to the F8F-1. The squadron lost its first Bearcat, F8F-1 BuNo 94928, on 13 May 1947 when its pilot ditched during dive bomb practice near Point Loma, CA. The squadron's first deployment with the Bearcat was aboard the USS Valley Forge (CV-45) to the Eastern Pacific from 1 September to 26 September 1947.

VF-11A deployed aboard the USS Valley Forge (CV-45) as part of Air Group Eleven for its world cruise from 9 October 1947 through 11 June 1948. The cruise commenced and ended from San Diego and made stops at Pearl Harbor, Sydney, Hong Kong, Tsingtao, Singapore, Trincomalee, RasTanura, Suez Canal, Gibraltar, Bergen, Portsmouth, New York, Panama Canal, and San Diego.

During the deployment two aircraft were lost. The first, F8F-1 BuNo 95393. was safely ditched near the Valley Forge on 3 December 1947. The second, BuNo 95204, went over the side while landing on 19 January 1948. Another F8F-1, BuNo 95312, piloted by LT D.G. Patterson, took the barrier and flipped over on its back on 19 January 1948.

After returning from the cruise, the squadron was redesignated VF-111 on 15 June 1948 and commenced a slow upgrade to the F8F-2. On 1 September, two pilots were killed when BuNos 95421 and 95304 collided off of La Jolla, CA.

As VF-111, the squadron made three short deployments aboard the Valley Forge with Bearcats before transitioning to the Grumman F9F-2 Panther. The first cruise was from 8 through 15 October 1948, during which carrier qualifications were conducted. This cruise, too, was not without mishaps. BuNo 95404 was damaged in a hard landing on 12 October 1948. The second cruise was from 29 March through 8 April 1949. During the third Bearcat cruise from 12 October through 15 November 1949, the squadron took part in Operation Miki Ex. VF-111 was disestablished on 19 January 1959.

Below, the CO OF VF-11A, CDR Howard W. Crews, in flight. (USN)

Above, VF-11A F8F-1 scratches for the wire aboard the Valley Forge in 1948 prior to a barrier engagement. (NMNA) Below, VF-11A F8F-1 BuNo 95312 was piloted by LT D.G. Patterson when it crashed on landing aboard the USS Valley Forge (CV-45) on 19 January 1948. (NMNA)

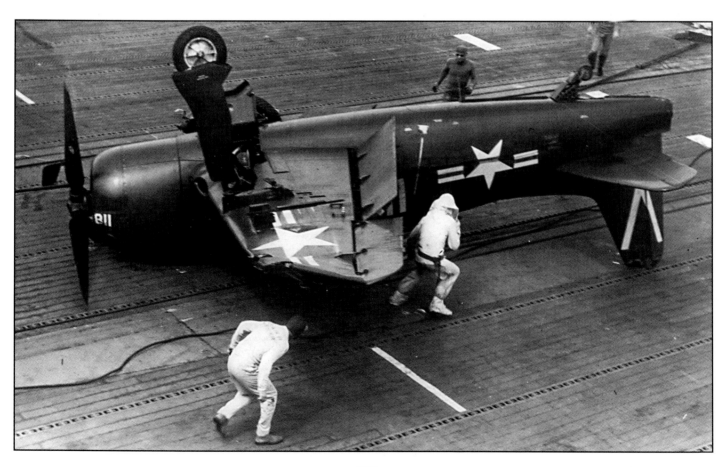

VF-112 was originally established on 9 April 1945 as VBF-11. The squadron was assigned the Grumman F6F Hellcat and was transferred to NAS Kahului, Maui, TH, in February 1946. The squadron was redesignated VF-12A in November 1946 and was reassigned to NAS San Diego, CA, on 31 January 1947 where they flew the F8F-1 Bearcat.

VF-12A deployed aboard the USS Valley Forge (CV-45) as part of Air Group Eleven for its world cruise from 9 October 1947 through 11 June 1948. The cruise commenced and ended from San Diego and made stops at Pearl Harbor, Sydney, Hong Kong, Tsingtao, Singapore, Trincomalee, RasTanura, Suez Canal, Gibraltar, Bergen, Portsmouth, New York, Panama Canal, and San Diego.

On 15 July 1948, VF-12 was redesignated VF-112. As VF-112, the squadron lost F8F-1 BuNo 95426 when it was ditched after take-off near NAS San Diego, CA. On 3 January 1949, F8F-2s started replacing the units F8F-1s. The squadron started transitioning to the Grumman F9F-2 Panther on 11 January 1950 and on 13 February the last F8F-2 Bearcat departed.

At top, four VF-12 F8F-2s in flight during the world cruise of VF-45. (USN) Above right, CV-45 at Bergen with VF-12 aircraft covered in snow. (USN) At right, VF-12 Bearcat is a backdrop during an emergency damage control drill on CV-45. (USN)

Above, VF-12A F8F-1s over the USS Valley Forge (CV-45) in 1947-1948. (USN via Tailhook) Below, the USS Valley Forge (CV-45) passing through the Suez Canal with VF-12A Bearcats on deck. Note the wide white fuselage stripes on 15 July 1948. (NMNA)

FIGHTER SQUADRON THIRTEEN, VF-13 "AGGRESSORS"

VF-13 was established on 2 August 1948 with assets from VF-1A/VF-11 and VF-2A/VF-12. The official squadron insignia recognizes this fact by including both squadrons' symbols. VF-13 received no aircraft of their own until mid-September and on 20 September was equipped with thirteen F8F-1s and three F8F-1Bs.

CVG-1 with VF-13 assigned conducted a world cruise on the USS Tarawa (CV-40) from 28 September 1948 through 21 February 1949. Only seven VF-13 Bearcats (six F8F-1s and one F8F-1N) were embarked to make room for VC-10's mixed bag of aircraft. During the cruise, F8F-1 BuNo 94964 was lost and the pilot was killed after a ramp strike on 2 October 1948. Another F8F-1, BuNo 94969, was lost when it was ditched successfully two miles east of Kaneohe, TH, on 10 October 1948. A third Bearcat, BuNo 95273, stalled on landing and sank on 30 November 1948.

VF-13 and Air Group One deployed to the North Atlantic aboard the USS Philippine Sea (CV-47) from 12 September through 22 November 1949. On 13 September 1949, BuNo 95402 crashed during bad weather near Berlin, PA, killing the pilot. While at sea, BuNo 95369's wing collapsed on landing on CV-47.

Immediately after the cruise, VF-13 started transitioning to the the F4U-5 Corsair and on 1 December 1949 had nine F8F-1s and eight F4U-5s. By January 1950, all the squadron's Bearcats had been replaced.

VF-13 Bearcat crashes into the barrier aboard the USS Philippine Sea (CV-47) in September 1949. (USN)

Above, CAG-13 F8F-1B BuNo 121509 belonged to VF-13A and was assigned to CDR D. C. Richardson during deployment aboard the USS Princeton (CV-37) in July 1948. Note thin red-blue-yellow tail stripe. (via Mark Aldrich) Below, VF-13A F8F-1B BuNo 121475 after a taxi accident while assigned to the USS Princeton (CV-37) in 1947/48. (Mark Aldrich collection)

VF-81 was established on 1 March 1944 at NAS Atlantic City, NJ, flying F6F Hellcats. The squadron transitioned to F4U-4 Corsairs before being redesignated VF-13A on 15 November 1946. The unit transitioned to F8F Bearcats and as VF-13A, made two short deployments with their F8F-1Bs. During carrier qualifications on 23 October 1947, BuNo 95468 was ditched successfully alongside the USS Tarawa (CV-40) when its engine failed. The first was aboard the USS Princeton (CV-37) from 9 through 14 May 1948. The second was from 9 through 21 July 1948 aboard the USS Valley Forge (CV-45). Both cruises were to the Eastern Pacific. On 2 August 1948, VF-13A became VF-131.

As VF-131, the squadron deployed once more aboard CV-37 from 1 October through 23 December 1948. Two aircraft were damaged during the cruise. The first, BuNo 122112, crashed on landing on 2 October. The second, BuNo 122105, was damaged when it took the barrier on CV-37 on 14 December 1948. The squadron transitioned to F4U Corsairs before becoming VF-64 on 1 December 1949. The squadron entered the jet age in December 1952 when they received the F9F-5 Panther.

At right, CV-37 in October 1948 with VF-132 Bearcats parked next to the island and with VF-131 Bearcats parked forward. (National Archives)

FIGHTER SQUADRON VF-14A/VF-132 "PEG-LEGGED-PETE"

VBF-81 was established on 13 May 1945 and equipped with F4U-4 Corsairs. The squadron was redesignated VF-14A on 15 November 1946 and transitioned to F8F-1B Bearcats. The unit lost its first pilot and aircraft on 4 February 1948 when BuNo 122138 failed to pull out on a strafing attack on a spar pulled behind the USS Boxer (CV-21). As VF-14A, the squadron made two short deployments in 1948. The first was from 9 through 14 May aboard the USS Princeton (CV-37) and the second was from 9 through 21 July aboard the USS Valley Forge (CV-45). On 12 July, BuNo 122117 was damaged after hitting the barrier on CV-45. The squadron was redesignated VF-132 on 2 August 1948.

As VF-132, they deployed again aboard CV-37 from 1 October through 23 December 1948. During this cruise, four aircraft, BuNos 122121, 122127, 122132 and 122136, were lost when they got lost while returning from a gunnery flight on 1 December 1948. Three of the pilots survived without injuries, but the fourth perished. Then, on 8 December 1948, the XO, LCDR Larry Flint, was leading another flight of Bearcats that became lost during a storm. One pilot ditched at sea and LCDR Flint circled the location for a while and ordered the remainder of the flight to land at Guam. Flint then headed toward Guam but ran out of fuel and ditched about 60nm south of the island in BuNo 122152. Another aircraft, BuNo 95221, was lost after he hit a target banner during air-to-air gunnery off Pontaverda, FL, on 20 March 1949.

VF-132 was disestablished on 30 November 1949.

Bottom, VF-13A (P/100) and VF-14A (P/200) Bearcats during carrier qualifications aboard the USS Tarawa (CV-40) in October 1947. (NMNA)

VF-15A

VF-151

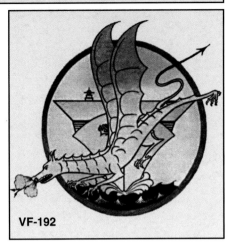

VF-192

VF-15A was established as VF-153 on 26 March 1945 and redesignated VF-15A on 15 November 1946. The squadron became VF-151 on 15 July 1948 and VF-192 on 15 February 1950. This was the second squadron designated VF-192 to fly the Bearcat (see VBF-19/VF-20A/VF-192). The squadron became VA-192 on 15 March 1956 and finally VFA-192 on 10 January 1986.

VF-15A started receiving F8F-1s in November 1947. F8F-1 BuNo 94887 swerved on take-off from NAS Seattle, WA, and caught fire on 11 May 1948. In July 1948, after being redesignated VF-151, the squadron began its transition to the F8F-2. The unit lost an F8F-1 when it was ditched during group tactics from NAS Alameda, CA, on 26 January 1949 and F8F-2 BuNo 122653 was lost when it went over the bow while landing on the USS Boxer (CV-21) on 25 January 1950.

As VF-192, the squadron took its F8F-2s aboard the USS Boxer (CV-21) on deployment to the Western Pacific from 11 January through 13 June 1950. The cruise included a short cold-weather arctic excursion. After returning from the cruise, the squadron transitioned to the F4U-4 Corsair. During the transition, F8F-2 BuNo 121536 and its pilot were lost during a midair with a USAF AT-6 during a glide bomb run near NAS Alameda, CA, on 18 July 1950. Another F8F-2, BuNo 122645, and its pilot were lost near Alameda when it hit a target banner and spun-in.

Below, VF-15A F8F-1 catches a wire on the USS Tarawa (CV-40) in June 1948. (Clay Jansson)

Above, VF-15A F8F-1 aboard CV-36 in 1948. Fin tip, rudder stripes and prop hub were red. (via Tailhook) Below, VF-151 F8F-2 Bearcats being loaded aboard the USS Boxer (CV-21) at NAS Alameda on 10 January 1950. The following month, while at sea, the squadron was designated VF-192. (via Corwin Meyer)

FIGHTER SQUADRON VF-16A/VF-152

VBF-153 was established on 26 March 1945 and flew F4U-1/4s and F6F-5s before being redesignated VF-16A on 15 November 1946. The squadron continued flying Hellcats until receiving F8F-1 Bearcats starting on 21 October 1947. The unit was redesignated VF-152 on 15 July 1948.

Although the squadron never deployed with its Bearcats, carrier qualifications were conducted. During one such CarQual, BuNo 95061 was damaged in a hard landing aboard the USS Antietam (CV-36) on 15 October 1948. A second hard landing occurred on the USS Valley Forge (CV-45) on 4 November 1948 to BuNo 94988. Another VF-152 F8F-1, BuNo 95234, overshot its landing at NAS Alameda, CA, on 6 December 1948, causing damage to the aircraft. BuNo 95317 was also damaged when it took the barrier aboard the USS Boxer (CV-21) on 10 January 1949. VF-152 started upgrading to the F8F-2 in May 1949. The squadron switched to the

Above, VF-16A F8F-1 BuNo 95006 on CV-40 off the coast of Southern California in July 1948. The squadron's fin tips were white. (Ed Baumgarten via NMNA) Below, VF-152 echelon with LCDR Rickabaugh in the foreground in BuNo 95272 followed by CDR Both in A/201, then A/214 and A/212. These four pilots and their aircraft won the gunnery meet at Alameda on 20 May 1949. (NMNA)

Douglas AD-4 Skyraider beginning on 1 December 1949.

On 15 February 1950, the designation was changed to VF-54. VF-54 became Attack Squadron Fifty-Four (VA-54) on 15 June 1956. The squadron was disestablished on 1 April 1958.

Above, VF-152 F8F-1 on CV-40 in 1948. (via Tailhook) Below, VF-16A F8F-1 (A/205) in foreground on CV-40 in July 1948. (Ed Baumgarten via NMNA) Bottom, VF-152 CAG bird BuNo 121701 at San Francisco on 30 October 1949. (Balogh via menard)

The second VF-17 was established on 1 August 1944 with the Grumman F6F Hellcat. The squadron transitioned to Chance Vought F4U-4 Corsairs in late 1945 and started receiving Bearcats in 1946. VF-17 was redesignated VF-5B on 15 November 1946. VF-5B was redesignated VF-61 on 28 July 1948 and transitioned to Grumman F9F-2 Panthers in early 1950.

On landing on CVB-41, BuNo 121547 took the barrier after it shed its hook on 14 October 1948. While deployed on CVB-41 in the Med on 22 November 1948, the engine quit

on VF-61 F8F-2 BuNo 121567 during a catapult shot and the aircraft sank along with its pilot. A wheels-up landing at NAS Norfolk, VA, slightly damaged F8F-2 BuNo 121645 on 29 December 1948. Another F8F-2, BuNo 121779, flew into the water killing the pilot off of NAAS Oceana on 28 November 1949.

While aboard the USS F.D. Roosevelt (CVB-42), F8F-2 BuNo 121673 was lost when it spun-in on landing on 14 February 1949. A week later, on 25 February 1949, BuNo 121677 was lost and its pilot killed when its wing tip came off during a

Above, VF-17 F8F-1 in 1946. (NMNA) Below, Jolly Roger F8F-2 BuNo 121664 on CVB-42. Note Jolly Roger insignia on the engine cowl. (via Menard)

glide bomb run and the pilot failed to pull out.

The Grumman F9F-2 Panther started to arrive at VF-61 in April 1950. On 22 May 1950, F8F-2 BuNo 121627 was lost when a wheels-up landing resulted in a fire at NAS New Orleans, LA.

Above, VF-61 F8F-2 BuNo 121636 prepares for a deck launch from the USS Coral Sea (CVB-43). (NMNA) At right, VF-61 F8F-2s prepare to deck launch from (CVB-43) on 14 September 1948. (NMNA) Below, VF-61's F8F-2s on deck of the Coral Sea on 26 March 1949. (NMNA)

FIGHTER SQUADRON VF-17A/VF-171 "ACES"

VF-82 was established at NAS Atlantic City, NJ, on 1 April 1944 and was redesignated VF-17A on 15 November 1946.

F8F-1 BuNo 94797 was ditched successfully off NAS Quonset Point, RI, on 25 April 1947. F8F-1B BuNo 95123 stalled on landing at NAAS Otis Field, MA, injuring the pilot on 12 June 1947. On 14 July 1947, the unit received its first FD-1 Phantom jet. The F8Fs soldiered-on with the FD-1s/FH-1s into 1949. On 11 August 1948, VF-17A was redesignated VF-171.

With VF-172 as part of CVG-17, the two squadrons made two short Caribbean deployments with the Phantoms prior to receiving the F2H-1 Banshee.

Below, VF-171 F8F-1B demonstrates a field catapult take off on 23 October 1948. Bottom, VF-171 F8F-1B BuNo 95281 on 23 October 1948. (Larry Smalley via D. Lucabaugh)

VGS-18 was established on 15 October 1942 and redesignated VC-18 on 1 March 1943 at NAS Whidbey Island, WA. Initially equipped with twelve FM-1 Wildcats and nine TBM Avengers, thirty-six F6F Hellcats were received in early 1944. During the war, the squadron was credited with 172 kills in the air and 300 planes destroyed on the ground. They were also involved in the sinking of the Japanese battleships Musashi and Yamato. They were known as the "Fickle Finger Squadron" because of the gesturing devil insignia. They were redesignated VF-18 in the summer of 1944 and moved to San Diego, CA, where they equipped with F8F-1 Bearcats. In October 1945, the squadron moved to NAS Quonset Point, R.I.

VF-18's first Bearcat deployment was aboard the USS Ranger (CV-4) from 30 September through 16 October 1945. The ship sailed from San Diego, CA, through the Panama Canal on the 11th of October and arrived at New Orleans on the 16th. CVG-18's aircraft, 45 F8F-1s and 15 TBM-3Es, flew ashore on the 15th and the remainder of Air Group 18 offloaded on 29 October 1945.

The first Bearcat fatality occurred on 22 March 1946 when the pilot of BuNo 94857 failed to pull out from a dive off Newport, RI. At an airshow in Omaha, NE, on 19 July 1946, F8F-1 BuNo 94954 crashed killing the pilot while attempting a slow roll right after take-off. In 1946, VF-18 took part in a shakedown cruise aboard the USS Leyte (CV-32) from 3 September through 12 December 1946. During the deployment, on 15 November 1946, VF-18 was redesignated VF-7A.

As VF-7A, the squadron made three short deployments aboard Leyte prior to its Med cruise. The first was for a Fleet exercise in the Atlantic from 3 February through 19 March 1947 as part of CVAG-7. The second cruise was from 3 April through 9 June 1947 and the third was a NROTC cruise from 7 through 25 July 1947. During this period, F8F-1 BuNo 95176 was damaged and its pilot injured in a hard landing on 6

Below, VF-18 F8F-1 BuNo 94853 at an East Coast base on 6 August 1946. (NMNA)

February. Another F8F-1, BuNo 95168, was damaged in a hard landing aboard CV-32 on 12 February 1947.

During the Leyte's Mediterranean deployment, from 30 July through 19 November 1947, VF-7A is credited with establishing the Centurion program (100 arrested landings on a given carrier) in November 1947. LCDR M.C. Norton Jr., CO of VF-7A, visited a British carrier in the Med and returned to the Leyte with the idea. LT Ben Parks designed the first patch and plaque and ENS Will Longley designed the first certificate. LTJG Larry Lawton became the first Centurion recipient on 8 July 1947. Also during the deployment, one Bearcat, BuNo 95075, was damaged on landing on 4 April 1947.

Between deployments, F8F-1 BuNo 95111 was damaged when it hit some trees during a forced landing due to fuel starvation on 26 December 1947. The pilot walked away with minor injuries. Then, during carrier qualifications on 20 January 1948, F8F-1 BuNo 95218 was damaged in a deck accident.

The squadron's last deployment as VF-7A was from 9 February through 19 March 1948. During the cruise, F8F-1s BuNos 95112 and 95189 were damaged during hard landings on 13 February 1948. VF-7A was redesignated VF-71 on 28 July 1948.

Two F8F-2s were lost during the VF-71 Caribbean training deployment from 28 August through 9 October 1948 Leyte. The first, BuNo 121568, stalled on landing on 28 August killing the pilot. The second, BuNo 121561, was ditched with gear down alongside CV-32 on 15 September. The squadron deployed a second time in 1948 to the North Atlantic for operation FLEETEX aboard CV-32 from 1 through 23 November 1948. BuNo 121542 ditched after take-off on 2 November 1948. The pilot was recovered uninjured. A second aircraft, an F8F-2P BuNo 121632, crashed into the water while landing on 19 November, killing

Above, CVG-7 CAG F8F-1 L/88 aboard the USS Philippine Sea (CV-47) in February 1949. CVG-7 was made up of VF-71, VF-72, VF-73 (all with F8F-1s), VC-4 with F6F-5Ns, and VA-115 with ADs. (USN) Below, VF-7A F8F-1s L/104, L/108, L/109, and L/118 prepare to launch from the USS Leyte (CV-32) on 5 September 1947. (NMNA)

the pilot.

CVG-7 and VF-71 were reassigned to the USS Philippine Sea (CV-47) for an emergency deployment to the Med due to the Berlin

Above, CVG-7 aboard CV-32 in 1948 with VF-7A Bearcat L/114 in the foreground. (NMNA) Below, VF-7A Bearcat BuNo 95203 chews the tail off its sister-ship, BuNo 95192, piloted by LT John Fisk during a taxi mishap on the USS Leyte (CV-32) on 8 July 1947. (NMNA) Next page top, VF-7A pilot CDR Gus Widhelm returns to Leyte in F8F-1 BuNo 95174 on 25 September 1947 after being "Zapped" for landing on the wrong carrier. (NMNA) Next page bottom, landing accident involving VF-7A F8F-1 L/121 piloted by LT Ben Parks aboard the USS Leyte (CV-32) on 3 June 1947. His hook was jammed and could not be lowered and he made a 3-point landing, bounced, sailed over the barrier and came to rest on the island. (NMNA)

Crisis from 4 January through 23 May 1949. During the cruise, F8F-1 BuNo 95165 was lost when it rolled off the deck during take-off on 11 January 1949, killing the pilot.

The squadron's last deployment with Bearcats was to the Med as part of MAG-11 aboard CV-32 from 6 September 1949 through 28 January 1950.

The squadron started to re-equip with Grumman F9F-2 Panthers in December 1949.

Above, VF-71 F8F-2 taxis down the deck of the USS Leyte (CV-32) while another VF-71 Bearcat is brought up on the elevator in late 1948. (NMNA) Below, VF-71 F8F-1s run engines prior to launching from CV-32 on 9 March 1947. (NMNA)

As VBF-18, the Hawks were flying F6F-3/5 Hellcats when established on 25 January 1945. They transitioned to F8F-1 Bearcats shortly thereafter and had a full complement of 24 aircraft by May 1945. The squadron encountered many teething incidents with their Bearcats. The first was a forced landing at Pendelton Hill, RI, on 8 December 1945. F8F-1 BuNo 94844 was damaged in a forced landing at NAS Quonset Point after an engine failure on 17 July 1946. Another pilot was injured when he flew into the ground on take-off near NAAS Hyannis, MA, on 9 August 1946.

VBF-18 participated in the shakedown cruise of the USS Leyte (CV-32) from August through December 1946. Once aboard ship the accidents continued. The pilot of BuNo 94949 put on a spectacular show when he did a torque roll into the water and sank while landing on CV-32 on 1 September 1946. Luckily, he was recovered uninjured. A VBF-18 pilot was killed when his wingtip failed on 30 September 1946 during dive training off CV-32 in F8F-1 BuNo 95110. Another pilot died when BuNo 94847 skidded off the deck during take-off from the USS Leyte (CV-32) on 15 October 1946.

When VBF-18 was reassigned from CVG-18 to CVG-7, they were redesignated VF-8A on 15 November 1946. Tragedy struck the squadron on 4 April 1947. Two pilots were killed during a midair between BuNo 95074 and 95162. Another Bearcat, F8F-1B BuNo 94987, was lost when it ditched successfully off the Leyte on 8 June 1947. Another F8F-1B, BuNo 95334, was damaged in a hard landing on CV-32 on 13 February 1948.

VF-8A became VF-72 on 28 July 1948 before being assigned to NAS Quonset Point, R.I. During this period, the squadron flew the Grumman F8F-1B/2 Bearcat. On 10 September 1949, F8F-1 BuNo 94765 was damaged when it swerved off the runway at Quonset Point. A pilot and aircraft were lost on 22 June 1950 when F8F-1B BuNo 95093 launched from the

Below, VBF-18 F8F-1 on CV-32 in late 1946. (NMNA)

Above, VBF-18 F8F-1 with "M" tail code above "18". (Howard Levy via Dave Lucabaugh) Below, VBF-18 starts its engines on the deck of the USS Leyte (CV-32) in 1946. Bearcat squadrons were large by today's standards, with VBF-18 having 24 F8F-1s assigned. 19 are visible in this photo. (NMNA)

USS Midway (CVB-41) for a ship-to-shore flight and disappeared. Another aircraft, BuNo 121463, was lost on 15 August 1950 when it spun-in on its base leg while landing on Midway. The pilot was recovered uninjured. Minor damage to F8F-1B BuNo 95310 occurred when its pilot made a forced landing near Quonset Point on 8 March 1951.

While flying Bearcats, the unit completed five carrier deployments. Three were aboard the USS Leyte (CV-32), the first as part of CVG-18 to the Caribbean and South America

At right, VBF-18 F8F-1 undergoing maintenance on the hangar deck of the Leyte during its shakedown cruise in 1946. (USN) Below, VBF-18 and VF-18 Bearcats on CV-32 in 1946. (USN)

from 16 September through 12 December 1946. The next two cruises were with CVAG-7 to the Med from 3 April through 9 June and from 30 July through 19 November 1947. A fourth deployment aboard CV-47 was

to the Med from 4 January through 23 May 1949. The last criuse aboard the USS Midway (CVB-41) was also to the Med from 10 July through 10 November 1950 as part of CVG-7

Above, VBF-18 Bearcats are on the right and VF-18 Bearcats are on the left during a visit to Valparaiso, Chile, aboard the USS Leyte (CV-32). Below, VF-8A F8F-1 in 1947/1948. Fin tip was white. (Fred Dickey via NMNA)

Above, VF-72 F8F-2 BuNo 121456 in 1948. (Dave Menard via NMNA) At left, VF-72 F8F-1B launches from the USS Leyte (CV-32) in March 1950 during Operation Port Rex. (via Tailhook) Below, VF-72 F8F-1B taxis forward aboard the USS Leyte (CV-32) on 9 March 1949. (NMNA)

VF-72 received its first F9F-2 on 16 March 1951. The squadron was redesignated VA-72 on 3 January 1956 and was disestablished on 30 June 1991.

Above, VF-8A F8F-1B being disconnected from the arresting gear after landing on the USS Leyte (CV-32) in 1947. (NMNA)
Below, VF-8A F8F-1B landing on the USS Leyte (CV-32) in 1947. (NMNA)

Above, VF-72 F8F-1 BuNo 95071 lands hot on the USS Philippine Sea (CV-47) on 16 January 1949. (NMNA) Below, VF-72 F8F-1B aboard CV-32 during Operation Frigid on 20 November 1948. (NMNA) VF-72 fin tips were white.

FIGHTER SQUADRON VF-19/VF-19A/VF-191 "SATAN'S KITTENS"

Above, VF-19 F8F-1 lands on the USS Corregidor (CVE-58) in August 1945. Below, VF-19 Bearcat with M33 yellow fuselage code in flight on 30 August 1945. (NMNA)

VF-19 was established on 15 August 1943 and was to become the first operational Bearcat squadron. On 14 April 1945, 10 enlisted men reported to Grumman for a thirty-day indoctrination course into the construction and mechanics of the F8F. They were followed by 25 pilots who left Santa Rosa, CA, on 18 May 1945 and by 26 more pilots and 11 enlisted men on 17 June 1945. The pilots received six days of training from engineers, test pilots, mechanics, and representatives from Pratt & Whitney, Aeroproducts propellers, and Sperry instruments before ferrying their new F8F-1s back to California.

While in training in California, BuNo 94794 was lost and the pilot, ENS Robert V. Clark, was killed while doing aerobatics near NAAS Vernalis. On 31 March 1945, the squadron participated in an air show

at Santa Rosa for the benefit of the Red Cross War Relief Fund. The squadron carrier-qualified aboard the USS Takanis Bay from 25-27 July 1945. Two separate simulated attacks were made against Army Coastal Defense installations in the San Francisco Bay area for the benefit of the Army.

On 2 August 1945, Air Group 19 boarded the USS Langley (CVL-27) at NAS Alameda for departure to Pearl Harbor. Arriving at Ford Island on 8 August, the squadron ferried its 37 Bearcats to Kahalui, Maui, on 9 August. On 24 August 1945, 27 pilots conducted carrier refresher training on the Langley. More carrier training was done on 28-30 August aboard the USS Corregidor (CVE-58). On the 30th, BuNo 94757 was damaged

when it took the barrier. The war ended on 2 September 1945.

Operations at VF-19 did not slow down with the end of the war. On 13 September 1945, VF-19 was operating from the USS Boxer (CV-21). The squadron returned to sea aboard the USS Hornet (CV-12) from 12-13 October and sailed for Alameda on 15 October arriving on 22 October 1945. Six days later, the Hornet and VF-19 departed California to return to Hawaii. They arrived at Oahu on 3 November 1945 and were off-loaded at NAS Barbers Point. While at Barbers Point, F8F-1s BuNos 94784 and 94789 collided and were lost near Barbers Point. Luckily, both pilots bailed out safely. Carrier qualifications were conducted aboard the USS Bennington (CV-20) on 22-23

January, 4-6 February, 26-27 February, 6-7 March, and 14-15 March 1946. Also on 28 February 1946, the unit conducted rocket firing training at Molokai.

The squadron was transported to Saipan aboard the USS Hancock (CV-19) from 18 March through 2 April 1946. The squadron embarked on the USS Antietam (CV-36) from 20 April through 20 August 1946 for a WESTPAC cruise, during which they took part in the Philippine Independence celebration.

On 15 November 1946, VF-19 was redesignated VF-19A. As VF-

Above, CO of VF-19 taxis his aircraft on the island of Saipan. (USN) Below, CO of VF-19 deck launches his F8F-1 from the USS Antietam (CV-36) on 11 April 1946. (NMNA)

19A, the squadron made five short

At left, Air Group 19 Bearcats being hoisted aboard ship. (USN) Below, CAG-19 with VF-19 Bearcats in the front row and VBF-20 Bearcats in the second row. Colorful CAG bird is in the foreground for this group photo at NAS Barbers Point, TH, in 1945. (USN)

---

deployments to EASTPAC. The first of these was aboard the USS Tarawa (CV-40) from 28 June through 25 July 1947. The other four were all aboard the USS Boxer (CV-21). The dates for these cruises were: 30 August through 29 September 1947; 29 October through 26 November 1947; 6 April through 27 May 1948; and 25 June through 17 August 1948.

While designated VF-19A, BuNo 94927 was lost and the pilot was killed when he dove into the sea off NAS Alameda during target practice on 18 August 1947. BuNo 95283 made a forced landing after take-off from NAS San Diego on 23 October 1947. Another F8F-1, BuNo 95365, was damaged during a hard landing on CV-21 on 12 November 1947. A wheels-up landing at NAF El Centro, CA, on 2 march 1948 damaged BuNo 95011. BuNo 95454 was damaged in a hard landing on CV-21 on 4 March 1948. Another F8F-1, BuNo 95415, was ditched off Boxer on 15 March 1948. Two F8F-1s, BuNos 95029 and 95458, were lost with their pilots after a midair on 17 March 1948.

VF-19A was redesignated VF-191 on 24 August 1948 and made four more deployments with Bearcats before transitioning to Grumman F9F-2 Panthers. Two cruises were made with F8F-1s and two with F8F-2s. The first two cruises were aboard CV-21 again and were conducted from 9 October through 21 October 1948 and from 1 November through 20 November 1948. The third deployment was aboard the USS Valley Forge (CV-45) from 30 July through 5 August 1949 and the fourth was from 12 August through 8 September 1949.

During the third Boxer cruise, VF-191 F8F-1N BuNo 94812 was damaged in a hard landing on 17 November 1948.

Three aircraft were lost in 1949, two to a mid-air during gunnery practice near Farallon Island on 5 January. Both pilots were killed in their F8F-1Bs, aircraft BuNos 95443 and 95326. While on CV-45, BuNo

138

Above, BuNo 95320 was Air Group Nineteen's CAG bird belonging to CDR E. E. Cook Jr. at NAS Alameda, CA, on 2 June 1947. Fuselage stripe was white and red. (William T. Larkins via D. Lucabaugh) Below, VF-19A F8F-1 CAG bird BuNo 95320 aboard the USS Boxer (CV-21) in 1947. (Bob Donaldson via Tailhook)

Above, VF-19A F8F-1 belonging to the squadron's commanding officer in early 1948 at Oakland, CA. (NMNA) At left, VF-191 F8F-1 on final in 1949. (via Tailhook) Below, VF-19A F8F-1 BuNo 95395 makes a flying trap aboard the USS Tarawa (CV-40) on 5 August 1947. (NMNA)

95045 was lost over the side when landing on 4 August 1949. F8F-1 BuNo 94941 hit the target banner and was forced to ditch off Alameda during a gunnery competition on 17 October 1949.

VF-191
"SATANS KITTENS"

At right, VF-191 F8F-2 (B/112) catches a wire on the USS Boxer (CV-21) in early 1950. The fin tip and prop hub were red. (NMNA) Below, VF-191's Commanding Officer's Bearcat aboard the USS Boxer (CV-21) in 1948.

Next page top, four VF-19A F8F-1s near San Diego two weeks prior to being redesignated VF-191. (NMNA) Next page bottom, VF-19A F8F-1s BuNos 95444 and 95434 in flight over San Diego, CA, on 5 August 1948. (NMNA)

FIGHTER SQUADRON VBF-19/VF-20A/first VF-192

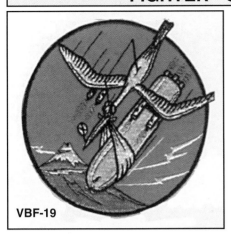

VBF-19

VBF-19 was established on 20 January 1945. F8F-1 BuNo 94791 crashed killing the pilot during a glide bombing run on Molokini Island 3 miles off Maui's south shore on 10 December 1945. While operating off the Bennington, BuNo 94894 ditched at sea on 27 February 1946. Another F8F-1, BuNo 94910, and its pilot were lost when it torque-rolled on landing on CV-36 on 5 June 1946. BuNo 94845 also was lost when it crashed and sank while circling the crash site. Three days later, BuNo 94885 was damaged in a barrier crash aboard CV-36. VBF-19 was redesignated VF-20A on 15 November 1946.

F8F-1 BuNo 94816 was lost and its pilot killed when it flew into a tree on the downwind leg while landing at NAAS Cotati, CA, on 29 January 1947. Another F8F-1, BuNo 94826,

VF-20A

At right, eight VF-20A F8F-1 Bearcats over San Francisco on 13 March 1947. The notches below the rudder were painted white. (National Archives)

143

was damaged in a forced landing at Lampson Field, Clear Lake, CA, on 11 February 1947. While operating aboard the Boxer, BuNo 94871 was damaged during a hard landing on 24 May 1948. VF-20A made five short deployments with their F8F-1s. The first cruise was from 28 June through 25 July 1947 aboard the USS Tarawa (CV-40). The next three were aboard the USS Boxer (CV-21) from 30 August through 29 September, 29 October through 26 November 1947 and from 5 April through 27 May 1948. The last was aboard the USS Princeton (CV-37) from 24 June through 20 August 1948. F8F-1 BuNo 95429 was ditched off the Princeton on 4 August 1948. VF-20A was redesignated VF-192 on 24 August 1948.

As VF-192 the unit deployed its F8F-1s three times aboard the Boxer from 9-21 October 1948, 1-20 November 1948, and 12 August

Below, VF-20A over San Diego on 13 March 1947 while assigned to the USS Valley Forge (CV-45). (NMNA)

FIGHTER SQUADRON VF-20A

Above, VF-20A F8F-1 BuNo 95318 at San Francisco Airport on 25 May 1947. Aircraft belonged to the squadron CO, LCDR D. C. (Whiff) Caldwell. (William T. Larkins via D. Lucabaugh) At right, same VF-20A F8F-1 launches from CV-37 on 13 August 1948. (NMNA) Below, VF-20A BuNo 95318 over San Fransisco on 2 June 1947. (William T. Larkins via D. Lucabaugh)

through 8 September 1949. A fourth deployment was aboard the USS Valley Forge (CV-45) from 30 July through 5 August 1949.

F8F-1 BuNo 94758 was lost when its pilot ditched off of NAS Alameda, CA, on 10 December 1948. The first VF-192 was redesignated VF-114 on 15 February 1950.

Above, VF-20A F8F-1 BuNo 95318 escorts a VA-20A AD Skyraider. (NMNA) Below, VF-20A F8F-1 BuNo 95364 prepares for a deck launch from CV-21 in 1947. (NMNA)

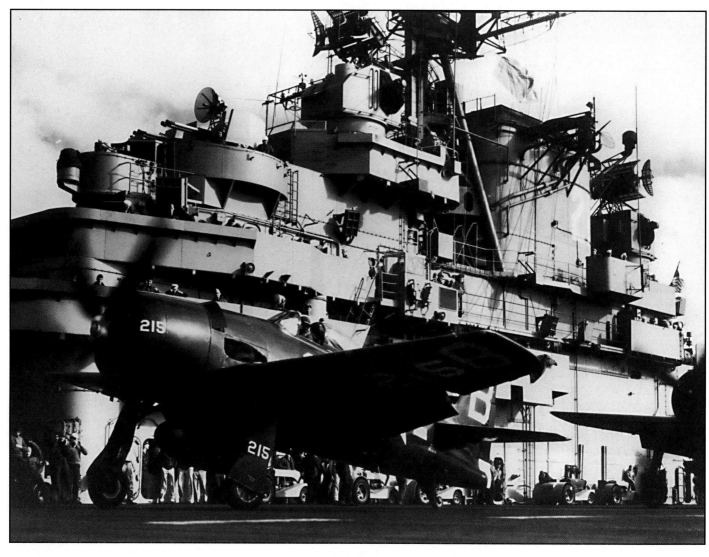

Above, VF-20A F8F-1 BuNo 95364 launches from the USS Boxer (CV-21). The area below the rudder was white. (NMNA) Below, VF-20A F8F-1 is being recovered after a night landing rollover accident at NAS Alameda, CA, on 8 December 1947. (USN)

Above, four VF-192 Bearcats in flight with belly tanks. (Bob Donaldson via Tailhook) Below, VF-192 F8F-1s prepare to launch from the USS Boxer (CV-21) in 1950 with a VF-732 (B/115) Bearcat at left. (NMNA)

FIGHTER SQUADRON VF-20/VF-9A/VF-91/VF-34 "BLUE BLASTERS"

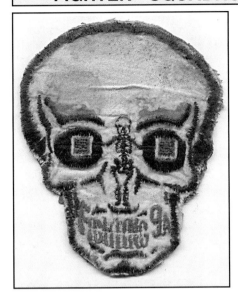

Above, VF-9A insignia was identical to the preceeding VF-20 one except that it said "Fighting 20". Below, VF-20 F8F-1 BuNo 95048 during CV-47's shakedown cruise in 1946. (NMNA)

VF-20 was established on 15 October 1943. Fighting Twenty operated the Grumman F6F-3/-5 Hellcat during World War Two. After the war, they operated from NAS Edenton, NC, from 26 June to 2 November 1945 when they moved to NAAS Elizabeth City, NC. In early 1946 VF-20 was transferred to NAAS Charlestown,RI, an auxiliary field to NAS Quonset Point where they transitioned to the Grumman F8F-1 Bearcat in April 1946. The squadron also operated a couple of F6F-5Ps alongside their Bearcats.

The first Bearcat arrived on 3 April 1946 and the squadron started carrier qualifications aboard the USS Salerno Bay in July. VF-20 was assigned to the USS Philippine Sea (CV-47) which was commissioned on 11 May 1946. On 27 September she commenced her shakedown cruise to the Caribbean and Guantanamo Bay. VF-20 pilots conducted live gunnery, bomb and rocket runs against targets on Culebra Island. Three carrier accidents occurred during this period. On 2 October, LTJG W.E. Scholz had a barrier crash and on 3 October LTJG D.C. Dolan made another barrier engagement due to a hook-up landing. On 14 november, LT H.E. VanNess lost his tailhook on landing and bounced over the barrier crashing into pack of aircraft spotted forward. Luckily, there were no injuries to the pilots or the ship's crew.

While on station, VF-20 became VF-9A on 15 November 1946. The squadron returned to base on 23 November and spent the rest of the year concentrating on night flying and instrument training. In January and

Above, VF-20 F8F-1 during a snow storm in 1946. (Dave Benton via NMNA) At left, VF-20 F8F-1 with squadron's insignia on the engine cowl. (via Tailhook) Below left, VF-9A F8F-1 nosed over on landing at NAAS Charleston. (Dave Benton via NMNA)

February 1947, the squadron trained in ground support with Army units in New Hampshire. They boarded CV-47 again on 28 March for another cruise to the Guantanamo Operations Area. VF-9A lost two planes during the cruise. ENS G.R. Hansen was killed when his plane crashed and burned at Leeward Point during FCLP in early April. The second Bearcat, BuNo 95038, was lost on 1 May when oil soaked brakes failed during taxi and it skidded over the side. In this case, the pilot was rescued without injury. The squadron returned to Rhode Island on 5 May 1947. They were at sea again the first week of June when they took part in a Midshipman Cruise aboard the USS Randolph (CV-15).

In late 1947, night carrier qualifications were conducted aboard the USS Kearsarge (CV-33). This was followed by a two-week trip to Guantanamo in January 1948. During the cruise three Bearcats, BuNos 95392, 95449 and 95490, were damaged during hard landings on CV-47 on 6 January 1948. VF-9A deployed to the Mediterranean aboard the Philippine Sea commencing on 9 February and ending on 26 June 1948. Once in the Med, VF-9A conducted extensive shore operations from Wheelus AFB in Tripoli.

On 12 August 1948, VF-9A became VF-91. The F8F-2 arrived on 3 December 1948. But this was not a good thing, as most were unflyable due to their condition and a parts shortage. The planes were received from VF-71 who took VF-91's well maintained F8F-1s to sea. VF-91 retained four flyable F8F-1s to use while the F8F-2s were returned to service.

In May 1949, ground support training was conducted followed by short deployments aboard the USS Leyte (CV-32), USS Kearsarge (CV-33), and the USS Midway (CVB-41). On 28 June, a Bearcat was lost when its pilot, LT Meryl Liams, crashed alongside the USS Kearsarge while attempting to land. LT Liams was rescued by an HO3S-1, one of the first

Above, VF-20 F8F-1 piloted by LT VanNess crashed in the pack after sheding its hook on on 2 October 1946. (via Tailhook) Below, VF-91 F8F-2 BuNo 121523 shed its right wing on CV-32 during a hard landing in rough seas on 31 January 1950. (via Tailhook) Bottom, VF-9A aircraft positioned on the forward deck of the USS Philippine Sea (CV-47) during its first Mediterranean deployment in 1948. (John Moore via Tailhook)

FIGHTER SQUADRON VF-9A "BLUE BLASTERS"

Above and at right, formation flight of VF-9A F8F-1s coded "PS" for the Philippine Sea in 1948. (NMNA) Below, VF-9A/VF-91 F8F-1 aboard the USS Philippine Sea (CV-47) in August 1948. VF-9A was redesignated VF-91 on 12 August 1948. (NMNA)

FIGHTER SQUADRON VF-91
"BLUE BLASTERS"

VF-91 F8F-1B BuNo 121529 piloted by LT M. A. Liams on 28 June 1949 stalled on approach, impacted the deck and crashed into the sea. Surprisingly, there were no casualties. (via Corwin Meyer)

VF-34

At right, imminent midair between a VF-92 (D/207) and a VF-91 (D/103) Bearcat. (NMNA) Below, VF-34 F8F-2 BuNo 122628 (K/401) in 1950 with "K" tail code of CVG-3. (NMNA)

helicopter rescues. For the remainder of the year, more training at sea was conducted aboard these three carriers as well as aboard the USS Saipan (CVL-48).

The squadron was redesignated VF-34 on 15 February 1950. VF-34 took part in Operation Portex aboard the USS Wright (CVL-49) from 18 through 24 March. This was followed by two carrier qualification cruises aboard the Wright and Philippine Sea. An F8F-2 was severely damaged when it hit the sea wall at NAS Quonset Point, RI, on 4 October 1950. On 1 November, sixteen VF-34 Bearcats flew to NAS Atlantic City for Operation Convex. The squadron received its first F9F-2 Panther on 27 November 1950. Eventually, 18 Panthers replaced the squadron's 24 Bearcats.

One of the first Bearcat squadrons was established as VBF-20 on 16 April 1945. While flying Bearcats, the squadron was stationed at NAS Charlestown, RI, and was assigned to CVG-9. The squadron took its F8F-1s aboard the USS Bennington (CV-20) for its Caribbean shakedown cruise from 30 September through 23 November 1946.

VBF-20 was redesignated VF-10A on 15 November 1946.

During carrier qualifications, VF-10A F8F-1 BuNo 95046's catapult bridle ring broke and it rolled off the

Above, VBF-20 F8F-1s in flight in 1946. (NMNA) Below, VBF-20 aircraft, some with 100lb bombs, on the deck of the USS Philippine Sea (CV-47) in 1946. BuNo 95836 (20BF58) has six kill marks on the side of the fuselage. (NMNA)

deck of CV-47 and sank in Narragansett Bay on 19 March 1947.

Above, VBF-20 F8F-1 makes 2,000th landing aboard the USS Philippine Sea (CV-47) in November 1946. (NMNA) At left, VBF-20 F8F-1 with bombs deck launches from the USS Philippine Sea (CV-47) in 1946. (NMNA) Below, VBF-20 F8F-1 20-BF-47 flipped on landing at NAAS Charleston. (Dave Benton via NMNA)

A short deployment was made to the Caribbean from 31 March through 5 May 1947 aboard the USS Philippine Sea (CV-47). The squadron lost F8F-1 BuNo 95208 and its pilot on 4 September 1947 when it stalled on landing at NAAS Charlestown. F8F-

Above, VF-10A F8F-1s run engines prior to deck launch from the USS Philippine Sea (CV-47) in the Mediterranean in early 1948. (NMNA) At right, VF-10A F8F-1 being hand spotted on the deck of the Philippine Sea. Fin tip was white. (USN) Below, this VF-10A F8F-1 was saved from a watery grave after a landing accident aboard the Philippine Sea (CV-47) in 1947. (NMNA)

Above, VF-10A Bearcat taxis at Philadelphia on 31 May 1947. (Dave Lucabaugh) Below, VF-10A F8F-2 near CV-47 in 1948. (John Moore via NMNA) Bottom, VF-10A F8F-1 demonstrates a ground catapult launch at Idlewild Airport, NY, in 1948. (NMNA)

1s BuNos 95087 and 95193 were lost with their pilots in a midair during a simulated attack on CV-20 on 18 November 1947.

During work-ups for its pending deployment, VF-10A lost F8F-1 BuNo 94895 when it was ditched off of CV-47 on 20 January 1948. F8F-1 BuNo 94811 was damaged in a deck accident on the USS Philippine Sea (CV-47) on 30 January 1948. Another Bearcat, BuNo 95252, was ditched off of CV-47 15 miles south of Malta on 27 May 1948 during CV-47's Med cruise from 9 February through 26 June 1948. F8F-1 BuNo 94782 was damaged and its pilot was injured during a forced landing after take-off from NAAS Charlestown on 9 August 1948. VF-10A was redesignated VF-92 on 12 August 1948.

VF-92 deployed to the North Atlantic aboard CV-47 from 22 October through 23 November 1948. During a short Caribbean training cruise, VF-92 F8F-2 BuNo 122696 was ditched off of the USS Midway (CVB-41) 23 miles from Nassau on 1 June 1949. VF-92 F8F-2 BuNo 121668 flew into the water during landing at NAS Quonset Point on 21 January 1950. The squadron was redesignated VF-74 on 15 January 1950.

As VF-74, the squadron made

Above and at right, VF-10A F8F-1 BuNo 95013 nosed-over at NAAS Charlestown in 1948. (NMNA) Below, two VF-74 F8F-2s run-up their engines prior to taxi and launch from NAS Quonset Point. in 1950. (USN via SDAM)

only one Bearcat deployment from 22 February through 14 March 1950 to the North Atlantic and the Caribbean and participated in Operation PORTREX. Prior to the deployment

Above, VF-92 F8F-2 on the Philippine Sea's elevator in October 1948 off of NAS Quonset Point. (NMNA) Below, VF-92 F8F-1 with engine running aboard the USS Philippine Sea (CV-47) in October 1948 off of NAS Quonset Point. (NMNA)

VF-74 F8F-2 BuNo 121527 was damaged in a hard landing on Leyte on 2 February 1950. Another VF-74 F8F-2, BuNo 121784, was damaged in a barrier landing on the USS Boxer (CV-21) on 19 February 1950 during work-ups for the cruise. Another Bearcat, BuNo 122630, was damaged in a hard landing on the USS

Leyte (CV-32) on 27 February 1950. On 1 March 1950, F8F-2 BuNo 121769 was also damaged during a hard landing on CV-32. VF-74 F8F-2 BuNo 121595 was severly damaged in a forced landing in the woods near NAS Jacksonville, FL, on 12 June 1950. Another F8F-2, BuNo 122673, was damaged during a forced landing

in a swamp on 30 June 1950.

Below, VF-74 F8F-2 BuNo 121565 deck launches from the USS Leyte (CV-32) in 1950. Note white propeller hub and forward tip of the belly tank (USN)

FIGHTER SQUADRON THIRTY - THREE, VF-33 "TARSIERS"

The second VF-33 was established on 11 October 1948 at NAS Quonset Point, RI. The squadron's first aircraft was the Grumman F8F-1B Bearcat. Carrier operations were conducted aboard the USS Leyte (CV-32) in January 1949 where F8F-1B BuNo 121469 was lost when it caught fire after crashing into the barrier and a 5" gun mount.

In February 1949, the squadron went aboard the USS Kearsarge (CV-

33). BuNo 121520 was ditched after take-off and the pilot was injured on 27 February 1949. On 22 February 1949, BuNo 95108 was lost off the bow of CV-32 when its catapult bridle broke on take-off. On 17 December 1949, the squadron transitioned to the Vought F4U-4 Corsair. LCDR H.H. Epes Jr.

was in command while the squadron was equipped with Bearcats.

Above and below, VF-33 F8F-1B BuNo 121469 piloted by LTJG L. E. Zeni sheds part of its wing on the 5" gun mount and catches fire aboard CV-32 on 19 January 1949. (NMNA)

FIGHTER SQUADRON FIFTY - THREE, VF-53 "BLUE KNIGHTS"

On 16 August 1948, under the command of LCDR W. D. Hubbell, the squadron was organized as part of Air Group Five with Grumman F8F Bearcats. 1949 brought a new Commanding Officer, LCDR W. R. Pittman, and a new aircraft, the Chance Vought F4U Corsair. VF-53 was redesignated VF-124 on 11 April 1958.

In late 1948, five performance tests were conducted between the F8F Bearcat and the FJ-1 Fury. The Bearcats involved were from VF-53 and VF-113 and the FJ-1s were from VF-51. The first test was from a standing start to 15,000ft and even though the water injection system on the Bearcats malfunctioned, the best F8F beat the best FJ-1 by over a minute. The second test was a zoom climb from 1,000 feet to 10,000 feet. This time the FJ-1 beat out the F8F by 13 seconds. For the third test a single VF-53 Bearcat raced a Fury to 25,000 feet with the FJ-1 arriving 1 minute and 40 seconds before the F8F. The fourth test was a simulated catapult launch climb performance test but was rendered inconclusive due to a timing error. The fifth test was a simultaneous take-off with the F8F getting off the ground and immediately pulling around and making a gunnery pass on the FJ-1 while it was still on the ground. A second pass was attempted and the F8F fell behind the rapidly accelerating Fury, arriving at 10,000 feet seven seconds after the Fury and at 15,000 feet 15 seconds behind the FJ-1.

PHOTOGRAPHIC COMPOSITE SQUADRON SIXTY - ONE, VC-61

Composite Squadron Sixty-One (VC-61) was based at NAS Miramar, CA, and was tasked with providing strike photographic reconnaissance services to the Fleet. Flying F6F-5Ps, F8F-2Ps, F4U-4P/5Ps, and later F9F-2P/5P Panthers and F2H-2P Banshees, the squadron would provide self-sufficient photo detachments to all Pacific Fleet carriers.

The squadron's Bearcats

Above, VC-61 F8F-2P in flight. (via Dan Rich) Below, VC-61 inspection at Miramar on 31 March 1950 with cameras displayed between a squadron F8F-2P and a PB4Y-1P. (National Archives)

PHOTOGRAPHIC COMPOSITE SQUADRON SIXTY - ONE, VC-61

deployed as detachments six times on Pacific Fleet carriers. These were: aboard CV-45 from 30 July through 5 August 1949; aboard CV-21 from 12 August through 8 September 1949; on CV-45 from 13-21 September 1949; on CV-45 from 12 October through 15 November 1949; and aboard CV-21 from 11 January through 13 June 1950.

VC-61 was established on 1 January 1949 and was redesignated VFP-61 on 2 July 1956. On 1 July 1959, VFP-61 became VCP-63 and then VFP-63 on 1 July 1961. VFP-63 was disestablished in May 1982.

Below, VC-61 F8F-2Ps near Miramar on 1 April 1949. BuNo 121583 is in the foreground. (USN)

COMPOSITE SQUADRON SIXTY - TWO, VC-62 "SHUTTER BUGS"

VC-62 was established on 3 January 1948 and its first insignia approved on 15 April 1949 reflected the squadron's mission. The "Shutterbug" standing on two carriers projected the image of the composite squadron delivering photographic services to the fleet. The nucleus of the squadron came from the FASRON Three Photo Unit at NAS Norfolk, VA. The first CO was CDR W.O. Moore who was assigned ten F9F-2Ps, two F4U-4Ps and four F4U-5Ps.

In the late '40s most air groups' photographic needs were met by four F6F-5P Hellcats assigned to the first fighter squadron or two each to the first and second fighter squadrons. Therefore the F8F-2P photo-Bearcat Detachments found their way onto only a handful of carriers before being

Below, VC-62 F8F-2P BuNo 121561 near NAS Norfolk in 1948. (NMNA)

replaced by F9F-2P/5Ps and F2H-2Ps. VC-62 began operating the F8F-2P in November 1948.

Six accidents occurred with Bearcats at VC-62. The first was on 4 May 1949 when BuNo 121689 ground looped on landing at NAS Norfolk. On 28 July 1949, BuNo 121584 took the barrier with injury to the pilot on the USS Franklin D. Roosevelt (CVB-42). Fatality struck

Above, VC-62 F8F-2P BuNo 121660 at NAS Norfolk, VA, on 23 May 1950. (NMNA) Below, VC-62 F8F-2P BuNo 121735. The squadron's original tail code was "TL" which was replaced with "PL" in 1951. (Lionel Paul via NMNA)

the squadron on 29 May 1950, when the pilot of BuNo 121686 flew into trees near Surry, VA. On 3 June 1950, BuNo 121663 spun-in near NAS Oceana during photo training, killing the pilot. On 1 July 1951, BuNo 121737 was ditched successfully alongside the USS Coral Sea (CVB-43). The last incident occurred on 12 November 1951 when BuNo 121758 was safely ditched near the USS Midway (CVB-41).

In late 1951 and early 1952, the Tarawa Det 32 with F8F-2P Bearcats cross-decked with the Midway Det's F2H-2Ps. After these two deployments, the photo Bearcat was retired from carrier usage as sufficent quantities of the more capable photo Banshees existed. VC-62 was redesignated VFP-62 on 2 July 1956.

VC-62 Bearcat detachments were: Det 6 aboard CVB-43 from 20 March through 6 October 1951; Det 8 aboard CV-34 from 15 May through 4 October 1951; Det 3 aboard CV-32 from 3 September through 20 December 1951; Det 5 aboard CVB-41 from 22 October through 15 November 1951; and Det 32 aboard CV-40 from 24 October through 18 November 1951.

Above, VC-62 F8F-2P BuNo 121270 over Task Force 201 and CV-32 in September 1951. (NMNA) Below, VC-62 F8F-2P at low level near CVB-41 on 14 November 1951. Note wide white fuselage and wing stripes. (NMNA)

Above, VC-62 F8F-2P BuNo 121737 in flight in 1950-51. (NMNA) Below, two VC-62 F8F-2Ps (PL/18 and PL/20) ready for a deck launch from the USS Oriskany (CV-34) in 1951. (NMNA)

VBF-17 was established on 2 January 1945. VBF-17 was redesignated VF-6B on 15 November 1946. The squadron became VF-62 on 28 July 1948 after having received its first F8F-2 on 30 June 1948.

With its Bearcats, VF-62 conducted a brief training cruise aboard the Coral Sea in September 1948. During Operation Seminole, VF-62 lost BuNo 121653 in a wave-off landing on 26 October 1948 on (CVB-41). F8F-2 BuNo 121612 while flying from Midway was ditched successfully fourteen miles from Guantanamo Bay on 29 October 1948. The squadron was reassigned to NAAS Oceana in November 1948.

In early 1949, the squadron was aboard the USS Kearsarge (CV-33) for a congressional demonstration cruise. Then VF-62 deployed its Bearcats to the North Atlantic aboard the USS F.D. Roosevelt (CVB-42) from 27 October through 23 November 1949. The Secretary of Defense, Louis Johnson, was aboard to monitor the operations. Prior to the deployment, one pilot and aircraft, BuNo 121481, was lost to a midair with an F4U-4 near NAAS Oceana, VA. Following the deployment, the squadron set a new Atlantic Fleet record of 13.85% during a fleet-wide gunnery competition.

Above, VF-62 F8F-2 rolls inverted and crashes into the sea off CVB-43 in September 1948. (via Norm Taylor) Below, VF-62 F8F-2 BuNo 121654 conducts a catapult launch from CVB-43 on 14 September 1948. (NMNA)

In early 1950, the F8F-2s were replaced with F8F-1Bs. Excellence in gunnery continued with a new record of 14.2% hits recorded and pilots received seven "E"s for gunnery, two "E"s for bombing, and one "E" for rockets. VF-62 deployed twice aboard the USS Leyte (CV-32) in 1950. The first time was for Operation

Above, VF-62 F8F-2s at the Cleveland Air Races in 1949. (P.M. Bowers via NMNA) At left, yellow-tipped VF-62 F8F-2 deck launches from CVB-42 during its arctic cruise in 1949. (Hank Winter via W. Thompson) Below, VF-62 F8F-2 BuNo 122626 at the Cleveland Air Races in 1949. (P.M. Bowers via D. Lucabaugh)

Portex and the second for Operation Camid. During the first cruise, F8F-1B BuNo 122104 was lost over the side of (CV-32) while landing on 8 March 1950. The pilot was recovered uninjured.

In August 1950, the squadron began its transition to the F2H Banshee. VF-62 was redesignated VA-106 on 1 July 1955.

VF-63 was established on 27 July 1948 at NAS Norfolk, VA, with the F8F-2 Bearcat. BuNo 121624 was damaged and the pilot injured on landing on CVB-43 on 22 September 1948. BuNo 121656 was ditched successfully on approach to CVB-41 on 14 October 1948. Another F8F-2, BuNo 121672, also was ditched on 1 March 1949 on take-off from CVB-42. Three shore accidents at NAAS Oceana occurred in 1949. BuNo 121639 made a gear-up landing, BuNo 122633 was ditched near base, and BuNo 121644 undershot its landing injuring the pilot. VF-63 deployed from 27 October through 22 November 1949 aboard CVB-42 to the North Atlantic.

The Bearcats were replaced with F4U-4 Corsairs in January 1950 before transitioning to Panthers in November 1952.

Above, VF-63 F8F-2 being loaded aboard CVB-42. (USN) Below, ten VF-63 (C/3XX) Bearcats run their engines in preparation of a deck launch aboard the USS F.D. Roosevelt (CVB-42) on 20 June 1949. The three Bearcats with white fin tips in the front of the pack belong to VF-61 (C/1XX). (USN)

FIGHTER SQUADRON VF-73

VF-73 was established on 27 July 1948 at NAS Quonset Point, RI, with F8F-2 Bearcats. In the spring of 1949, the F8F-2s were replaced by F8F-1s. F4U-4 Corsairs started replacing the Bearcats in the spring of 1950 and the squadron flew a mixed bag of Corsairs and Bearcats until the Grumman F9F-5 Panther was received in November of 1951.

F8F-1 BuNo 95332 and its pilot were lost 3 miles off Sakannat Point, RI, when it dove into the sea on 8 September 1949. Another F8F-1, BuNo 95358, caught fire while taxiing at NAS Quonset Point, RI, on 22 November 1949.

The unit made three short cruises. Two were aboard CV-32 from 28 August through 9 October to the Caribbean and from 1-23 November 1948 to the North Atlantic. The third cruise was aboard CV-47 from 4 January through 23 May 1949 in response to the Berlin Crisis.

Above, VF-73 F8F-2 in 1948. Fin tip flash was blue. (NMNA) Below, VF-73 F8F-2 tensioned for a catapult launch from the USS Leyte (CV-32) in October 1948. (NMNA)

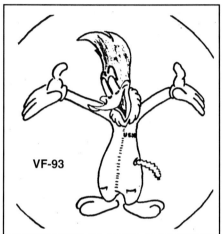

VF-93

FIGHTER SQUADRON EIGHTY, VF-80 "VIPERS"

VF-80 was established on 1 February 1944 as part of CVG-80 and was equipped with Grumman F6F-5 and F6F-5N Hellcats. After the war, the squadron transitioned to the Grumman F8F-1 Bearcat in January 1946.

With Bearcats, the squadron sailed to the Philippines aboard the USS Hancock (CV-19) from 18 March through 3 April 1946 where they were offloaded to take part in the Philippine Independence celebration. After the event, VF-80 loaded aboard the USS Boxer (CV-21) and deployed to the Western Pacific from 20 April through 10 September 1946.

VF-80 was disestablished on 16 September 1946. Its Bearcats were coded with 80-F-XX on the fuselage sides.

FIGHTER SQUADRON NINETY - THREE, VF-93

VF-93 was established on 12 August 1948 and flew the F8F-1/2 until disestablished on 30 November 1949. The squadron's aircraft were coded D/3XX.

The squadron deployed once aboard the USS Philippine Sea (CV- 47) from 22 October through 23 November 1948.

On 25 February 1949, F8F-2 BuNo 121544 spun-in on landing aboard the USS Leyte (CV-32) killing the pilot.

FIGHTER SQUADRON VF-113 "STINGERS"

VF-113 was established on 15 July 1948 with the F8F-1 Bearcat at NAS North Island, CA. The squadron switched to the F8F-2 on 28 March 1949 and acquired F4U-4B Corsairs on 9 March 1950. The Stingers made two combat cruises aboard the USS Philippine Sea (CVA-47) with their Corsairs before receiving F9F-5s in October 1952.

In late 1948, five performance tests were conducted between the F8F Bearcat and the FJ-1 Fury. The Bearcats involved were from VF-53 and VF-113 and the FJ-1s were from VF-51. The first test was from a standing start to 15,000ft and even though the water injection system on the Bearcats malfunctioned, the best F8F beat the best FJ-1 by over a minute. The second test was a zoom climb from 1,000 feet to 10,000 feet. This time the FJ-1 beat out the F8F by 13 seconds. For the third test a single VF-53 Bearcat raced a Fury to 25,000 feet with the FJ-1 arriving 1 minute and 40 seconds before the F8F. The fourth test was a simulated catapult launch climb performance test but was rendered inconclusive due to a timing error. The fifth test was a simultaneous take-off with the F8F getting off the ground and immediately pulling around and making a gunnery pass on the FJ-1 while it was still on the ground. A second pass was attempted and the F8F fell behind the rapidly accelerating Fury arriving at 10,000 feet seven seconds after the Fury and at 15,000 feet 15 seconds behind the FJ-1.

In the summer of 1949, F8F-2 BuNo 121705 was ditched off San Diego during gunnery tow duty.

Above and previous page, VF-113 F8F-2 BuNo 122616 on 4 July 1949 at the Santa Monica Airport while assigned to the Valley Forge. Note the 500lb bomb and rockets mounted to the wing. The fin tip was blue. (William Swisher)

FIGHTER SQUADRON ONE THIRTY-THREE, VF-133

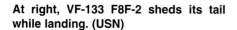

VF-133 was established on 2 August 1948 and flew the F8F-1B Bearcat. The squadron made one deployment aboard the USS Princeton (CV-37) as part of CVG-13 to the Western Pacific from 1 October through 23 December 1948. VF-133 was disestablished on 31 October 1949.

At right, VF-133 F8F-2 sheds its tail while landing. (USN)

FIGHTER SQUADRON VF-153/VF-194 "THUNDERCATS"

VF-153 was established on 15 July 1948. In 1948, barrier crashes were quite common at VF-153. The first occurred in September aboard the USS Valley Forge (CV-45) when an F8F-1 piloted by ENS Westmorland ended up inverted.

LTJG Crenshaw was injured when he took the barrier in F8F-1 BuNo 95345 aboard the USS Antietam (CV-36) on 11 October 1948. Another F8F-1, BuNo 95004 piloted by ENS Al Rappview, was damaged in a barrier landing on the USS Valley Forge (CV-45) on 26 October 1948. The pilot of F8F-1B BuNo 121504 was injured when the aircraft's tail broke off on landing on the USS Princeton (CV-37) on 28 November 1948. F8F-1 BuNo 95294 was ditched successfully by its pilot in San Francisco Bay on 8 December 1948. VF-153 F8F-2 BuNo 122624 was damaged during a hard landing on the USS Boxer (CV-21) on 14 January 1950. The same day, another F8F-2, BuNo 122684, was damaged when it took the barrier. This was followed by a hard landing in F8F-2 BuNo 122703 on 16 January 1950.

VF-153 was redesignated VF-194 on 15 February 1950. The squadron deployed its F8F-2s aboard the USS Boxer (CV-21) from 11 January through 13 June 1950. While flying from Boxer on 31 May 1950, the pilot of F8F-2 BuNo 122657 was killed when he stalled and crashed on landing. In August 1950, the squadron started to transition to the Vought Corsair. VF-194 was redesignated VA-196 on 4 May 1955.

Below, VF-153 Bearcat piloted by LTJG Willie Crenshaw crashed on landing aboard the USS Antietam (CV-36) and ended up inverted on 11 October 1948. (NMNA)

Above, VF-153 F8F-1 piloted by ENS Art Westmorland took the barrier aboard CV-45 and ended up on his back in September 1948. Below, VF-153 F8F-1 BuNo 95004 piloted by ENS Al Rappview lost its left wing tip when it took the barrier on CV-45 after the hook broke on 26 October 1948. (NMNA)

176

Above, three VF-153 F8F-2s prepare to launch from the USS Boxer (CV-21) on 9 June 1949. (National Archives) Below, VF-194 F8F-2s in the right foreground (B/4XX) with Bearcats from VF-193 (B/3XX), VF-192 (B/2XX) and VF-191 (B/1XX), aircraft assigned to Air Group Nineteen, aboard the USS Boxer (CV-21) in June 1950. (NMNA)

Above, VF-194 and VF-193 Bearcats run-up with British Fireflies on the USS Boxer (CV-21) on 6 March 1950. (NMNA) Below, three VF-194 Bearcats in the foreground, B/4XX with VF-193 B/3XX, and VF-192 B/2XX, further up the deck on CV-21. (NMNA)

Above, orange-trimmed VF-194 F8F-2 BuNo 695 with engine running is being raised on the deck edge elevator for take-off on the USS Boxer (CV-21) in 1950. (USN)

FIGHTER SQUADRON VF-173 "JESTERS"

VF-173 was established on 11 August 1948 at NAS Quonset Point, RI. The squadron was commanded by LCDR D.H. Nedda and was equipped with sixteen F8F-1Bs and one SNJ. The unit's 25 pilots attended ground school, and used link trainers for instrument training prior to conducting carrier qualifications aboard the USS Kearsarge (CV-33) in December 1948 and January 1949. After carrier qualifications were completed, the squadron traded in their Bearcats for F4U-5 and later F4U-4 Corsairs.

On 30 November 1948, the pilot of BuNo 121470 was injured when he stalled after a wave-off from NAAS Charlestown, RI.

Below, VF-193 F8F-2s operating on the USS Boxer (CV-21) in 1948. (USN)

FIGHTER SQUADRON VF-193 "GHOST RIDERS"

VF-193 was established on 24 August 1948 with F8F-1s and assigned to the USS Boxer (CV-21). Three days later, the gear retracted during the take-off roll of BuNo 94838 at NAS Alameda, CA. During operations from Boxer, BuNo 95470 was lost when it was ditched successfully on 1 November 1948.

After receiving F8F-2s, BuNo 121622 was damaged when it stalled on landing at NAAF Fentress Field,

VA. The squadron took its Bearcats aboard Boxer four times. The first deployment was from 9-21 October 1948. The second was from 1-20 November 1948 and the third was from 12 August through 8 September 1949. The last cruise was from 11 January through 13 June 1950, after which the unit began its transition to the F4U-4 Corsair. The squadron also

deployed aboard the USS Valley Forge (CV-45) from 30 July through 5 August 1949.

Above, VF-193 F8F-1 BuNo 95280 being hoisted aboard the USS Boxer. (via Tailhook) Below, VF-193 F8F-1 taxis on USS Boxer (CV-21) in 1948. (via Tailhook)

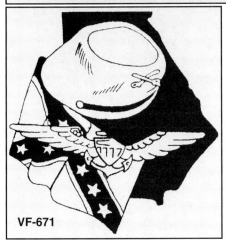

VF-671

FITRON 81

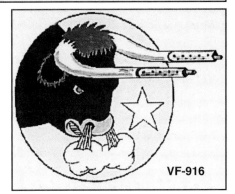

VF-916

VF-921

In April 1951, Air Group Eight was established from four reserve fighter squadrons: VF-671 (E/100), VF-742 (E/200), VF-916 (E/300), and VF-921 (E/400), and one attack squadron VA-859. All four fighter squadrons would operate Bearcats before being augmented into the regular Navy and being redesignated VF-81 (VF-671), VF-82 (VF-742), VF-83 (VF-916), and VF-84 (VF-921) on

Below, VF-742 F8F-2 BuNo 121611 (E/212) and 122629 (E/204) prior to a mission from Midway in August 1952. (Don Walsh via D. Lucabaugh)

4 February 1953.

VF-671: Reserve squadron VF-671 was called to active duty on 1 February 1951 at NAS Atlanta, GA, with the F4U-4 Corsair. A Mediterranean deployment was conducted aboard the USS Tarawa (CV-40) from 28 November 1951 through 11 June 1952. After returning to CONUS, the squadron was based at NAAS Oceana and transitioned to the F8F-2 Bearcat. In December 1952, the Grumman F9F-5 was received. On 4 February 1953, VF-671 was redesignated VF-81.

VF-742: Reserve squadron VF-742 was called to active duty in February 1951 and was initially equipped with F4U-4 Corsairs. In January 1952, the F9F-2 Panther replaced the Corsairs for a few months before being replaced by F8F-2 Bearcats in June. The Iron Men started transitioning to the F9F-5 in September 1952 and completed the transition in November. On 4 February 1953, VF-742 was redesignated VF-82 and in early 1954, the squadron transitioned to the F2H-2B/2N Banshee.

VF-916: Reserve squadron VF-916 was called to active duty in response to the Korean conflict on 1 February 1951 with F4U-4 Corsairs. In December, the squadron received the Grumman F9F-2 Panther, but reverted back to props with the Grumman F8F-2 Bearcat in May 1952. In September, VF-916 returned to jets with the F9F-5 Panther. On 4 February 1953, the squadron was redesignated VF-83.

VF-921: Reserve squadron VF-921 was called to active duty from NAS Saint Louis, MO, in February 1951. They flew the F4U-4 Corsair and transitioned to the F8F-2 Bearcat in June 1952. They started transitioning to the F9F-5 Panther in September 1952 and completed the transition in November. In February 1953, VF-921 was redesignated VF-84.

Below, VF-742 F8F-2 BuNo 121635 aboard the USS Midway (CVB-41) in August 1952. The aircraft's vertical fin tip was white. (Don Walsh via D. Lucabaugh)

TRAINING COMMAND BEARCATS, IATU, ATU-2, ATU-100

The Bearcats first use as an advanced trainer appears to have been with the Instructor Advanced Training Unit (IATU) at NAAS Corpus Christi, TX. In February 1948, the unit had five F8F-1s assigned along with eight F4U-4s, six SNJs and three SNBs.

Above, unmarked Instructor Advanced Training Unit (IATU) F8F-1 BuNo 95241 taxis at NAAS Cabaniss in early 1949. (NMNA) Below, ATU-2 F8F-1 at top poses with (in descending order) ATU-4 Hellcat, ATU-1 Hellcat, and ATU-5 Skyraider near NAAS Cabaniss Field on 31 October 1951. (via Tailhook)

IATU was joined by ATU-2 (VF-ATU-2) which was established on 15 November 1948 at Cabaniss Field, TX. The squadron flew both F8F-1 Bearcats and F6F-5 Hellcats. The squadron retired its Hellcats in June 1950. The Hellcat had been utilized in the advanced training command for almost eight years and the last seven students completed training on 9 June 1950. In May 1952, the unit transferred to NAAS Kingsville, TX, and was redesignated ATU-100 in late 1952. The Bearcats were used for three years until ironically being replaced by F6F Hellcats again in late 1953.

Above, Link trainer used during advanced flight training in the F8F at NAS Corpus Christi, TX, in July 1949. (National Archives via Tailhook) Below, four ATU-2 F8F-1s BuNos 94900 (MB/222), 95107 (MB/221), 95202 (MB/223), and 95333 (MB/224), on 25 April 1951. (NMNA) At right, six ATU-2 F8F-1 Bearcats in flight in 1949 near their base in Texas. (NMNA)

ATU-100

Above right, ATU-100 F8F-1 BuNo 95008 at NAAS Kingsville South Field in January 1952. (Bob Donaldson via Tailhook) At right, ATU-100 student heads towards his mount, F8F-1 BuNo 95263, in early 1953. (Bob Donaldson via Tailhook) Below, ATU-100 F8F-1 at Kingsville, TX. (NMNA)

ATU-100 AND THE FRENCH CONNECTION

Above, F8F-1 flown by the French at ATU-100 prior to their assignment to French Indochina. (via S. Nicolaou) Below, two French officers pose next to a ATU-100 Bearcat. (via S. Nicolaou)

Above, ATU-100 F8F-1 BuNo 95167 taxis out for a training flight in early 1953. (Bob Donaldson via Tailhook) Below, ATU-100 Bearcat ramp with unit preparing for a formation training exercise. (Grumman) Bottom, seven ATU-100 F8F-1 Bearcats during formation training over southern Texas. (Grumman)

PENSACOLA-BASED CARRIER QUALIFICATION TRAINING UNIT CQTU-4

As can be imagined, when you put such a high performance aircraft as the Bearcat in the hands of novice pilots especially during carrier training, you're asking for trouble. This is what happened at CQTU-4. The following heavy losses were recorded with the unit.

CQTU-4 F8F-1 BuNo 95246 was ditched wheels-down off the runway into Perdido Bay on 12 August 1949. During carrier trials aboard the USS Cabot (CVL-28), BuNo 95054 was damaged when it took the barrier after a hard landing on 29 August 1949. The pilot of BuNo 95236 was injured after hitting trees on landing at Bronosn Field, FL, on 14 January 1950. During carrier qualifications on 13 February 1950, BuNo 95495 flew the water while landing on Cabot. BuNo 94779 was destroyed and its pilot killed when it spun-in on landing at NAAS Barin Field, AL, on 12 April

1950. A CQTU-4 pilot was killed when he spun-in during landing on the USS Wright (CVL-49) in BuNo 95496 on 7 November 1950. On 22 November 1950, BuNo 94862 was severly damaged after hitting the trees at ALF Barin Field. BuNo 94874 was damaged when it stalled on landing at Barin Field on 13 February 1951. At NAAS Corry Field, FL, BuNo 94883 was lost and its pilot was killed when it spun-in on 4 February 1951. BuNo 94903 ground looped during landing at NAAS Corry Field, FL, on 4 March 1951. Another pilot was killed on 26 March 1951 when he stalled BuNo 94923 at Barin Field. BuNo 94891 stalled on landing at Barin Field and

Above, F8F-1 during advanced carrier qualifications aboard the USS Cabot (CVL-28) on 14 July 1952. (via Tailhook) Below, CQTU-4 F8F-1 BuNo 95434 at NAAS Corry Field, FL, in 1952. (via Tailhook)

hit inverted, killing the pilot on 22 May 1951. BuNo 94807 stalled on landing at Barin Field with minimum damage on 5 July 1951. Another F8F-1 was damaged on landing at Barin Field on 18 October 1951. A CQTU-4 F8F-1, BuNo 95375, was lost and the pilot was killed he when spun-in on landing at NAAS Bronson Field, FL, on 21 April 1952.

CQTU-4

Above, CQTU-4 F8F-1 BuNo 94768 at NAAS Saufley Field, FL, in 1952/53. (via Tailhook) At right, CQTU-4 F8F-1 BuNo 95223 from NAAS Corry Field, FL, traps aboard the USS Cabot (CVL-28) in 1952. (J. T. Ferrell via Tailhook) Below, CQTU-4 F8F-1 during carrier qualifications aboard the USS Monterey (CVL-26) on 7 April 1952 with the Secretary of Defense observing the operations. (via Tailhook)

Above, CQTU-4 F8F-1 BuNo 94862 hit a tree at Barin ALF on 22 november 1950 and was trucked back to its base, Corry Field for salvage. (NMNA) Below, CQTU-4 F8F-1 BuNo 95076 during carrier qualifications aboard the USS Monterey in March 1951. (E.W. Quandt via Dave Menard)

FRENCH at CQTU-4

Above, damaged CQTU-4 F8F-1 being off-loaded after a mishap during carrier qualifications with the French contingent. (via S. Nicolaou) At left and below, CQTU-4 F8F-1 coded "BA" during French carrier qualifications in the Gulf of Mexico. (via S. Nicolaou)

The Naval School of Photography was part of the Naval Air Technical Training Unit (NATTU) at Pensacola, FL. The F8F-2P Bearcat was utilized at the school from 1949 through 1952 before being replaced with F9F photo Panthers and photo Cougars.

At right, NATTU F8F-2P Bearcats at NAS Pensacola, FL, in 1949. Rudder and outer wings were international orange. (Bill Crimmins via NMNA) Below, French students pose in front of a taxiing NATTU F8F-2P. Rudder and outer wing trim was international orange. (via S. Nicolaou)

Above, CIC school F8F-2 VW/402 after a landing mishap at NAS Glenview, IL, in September 1951. (Clay Jansson) NACA/Ames Bearcat test ship fitted with a very large paddle-blade prop in 1947. (NACA/Ames via Mike O'Conner/Tailhook)

NATIONAL ADVISORY COMMITTEE FOR AERONAUTICS, NACA AMES

MARINE BEARCATS

The Marines used Bearcats as advanced trainers in 1951-52 on the East Coast at MCAS Quantico, VA, and MCAS Cherry Point; on the West Coast they were used at MCAS El Toro, CA. The Quantico-based unit was AES-12. Cherry Point had VMT-1 and VMFT-20 and El Toro had MTG-10, VMT-2, and VMFT-10.

Two known Marine losses occurred: An AES-12 pilot was lost on 26 October 1951 when F8F-2 BuNo 121670's wing failed during dive training at MCAS Quantico, VA. A VMFT-10 F8F-2 BuNo 121764 was lost to a fire-in-flight near NAAS El Centro, CA, on 19 February 1952. The injured pilot bailed out and was successfully recovered.

Above. rare USMC usage of the Bearcat was at VMFT-10 at MCAS El Toro, CA, in 1951. New fighter pilots would fly three hops in the SNJ and the rest in these F8F-1s. (Gene "Mule" Holmberg) Below, AES-12 F8F-2 assigned to MCAS Quantico, VA. (Clay Jansson)

Above and below, AES-12 F8F-2 BuNo 121553 landing at MCAS Quantico, VA. (USMC) Bottom, AES-12 F8F-2 BuNo 121683 on take-off roll at MCAS Quantico. (USMC)

At right, Anacostia reserve F8F-1 BuNo 94911 preparing to start its engine. (Dave Lucabaugh) Below right, one of the first Anacostia-based F8F-1s. Note Anacostia has not been applied to the fuselage side as yet. (via Dave Lucabaugh) Bottom, Anacostia reserve F8F-1 BuNo 95291. (Dave Lucabaugh)

Bearcat squadrons at NAS Anacostia were VF-662, VF663, and VMF-321. For their annual two-week training cruise, the Navy squadrons VF-662 and VF-663 trained at MCAS Miami in the summer of 1952.

VMF-321 was established on 1 July 1946 with F4Us and received Bearcats in 1949. They received Corsairs once again when their F8Fs were shipped to the French in Indochina in 1953.

In 1951, the squadron was put on alert due to the Korean War. However, the squadron did not deploy as a unit. Instead, pilots were sent to Korea as replacements to augment regular Marine squadrons already deployed.

Three F8Fs were involved in

NAVAL RESERVE

The US Naval Reserve received the F8F-1 and F8F-2 Bearcats from 1950 through 1953. The hot little fighter flew alongside Hellcats, Corsairs, Phantoms, Banshees and Panthers before being withdrawn from service. Eight Reserve Air Bases are reviewed here: NAS Anacostia, NAS Birmingham, NAS Denver, NAS Glenview, NAS Olathe, NAS Norfolk, NAS St. Louis, and NAS Spokane. In 1952-53, significant numbers of F8Fs were assigned to Niagara Falls (19), Seattle (33), Jacksonville (18), and Lincoln (16). However, it is not clear if these were ever operational.

NAVAL AIR RESERVE NAS ANACOSTIA, DC

Above and below, VMF-321 during gunnery training at Webster Field on 22 August 1952. (National Archives)

Above, Anacostia-based F8F-1 BuNo 95350 in May 1951. (via Norm Taylor) Below, three Anacostia-based F8F-1s over Washington DC. BuNo 95343 is in the foreground (A/21). The wide fuselage stripes were international orange. (NMNA)

At right, four Anacostia-based F8F-1s piloted by VF-662 and VF-663 fly along Miami Beach, FL, in the summer of 1952 during their cruise with VMF-321 to MCAS Miami. (USN)

mishaps. VMF-321 F8F-1s BuNo 94881 and 94888 were ditched 15 miles off Patuxent River, MD, after a midair on 12 December 1950, and BuNo 95343 made a forced landing at Andrews AFB, MD, on 25 February 1951.

NAVAL AIR RESERVE NAS BIRMINGHAM, AL

NAS Birmingham was established on 15 October 1948 and was disestablished on 1 October 1957.

Above, Birmingham-based Bearcat after shredding its horizontal tail feathers in a high speed dive in early 1951. (USN) Below, Birmingham Reserve F8F-2 BuNo 121712 was recovered after a crash on 26 July 1952. (NMNA)

NAVAL AIR RESERVE NAS OLATHE, KS

Olathe, a training and transport squadron base during WWII. became a Reserve Air Station in 1946. VMF-215, VF-882 and VF-884 flew Bearcats with over 40 F8F-1s assigned. The Bearcats flew along side FJ-1 Furys and were replaced by Grumman F9F Cougars.

On 13 May 1950, F8F-1 BuNo 94917 was damaged during a torque roll on landing at NAS Olathe, KS.

Another Bearcat was lost when a VMF-215 pilot was killed when he dove-in near Schell City, MD.

Below, Olathe-based F8F-1 BuNo 95256 at NAS Glenview in September 1950. (Clay Jansson via Fred Roos) Bottom, maintenance crew fuels Olathe-based F8F-1 BuNo 95268. (Roger Besecker)

Olathe-based pilot carrier qualifies in F8F-1 Bearcat BuNo 95308. (NMNA)

NAVAL AIR RESERVE NAS DENVER, CO

Buckley Field, Denver, CO, was established in January 1947. The station's fighter squadrons were originally assigned F6F-5 Hellcats and F4U Corsairs. The F8F-2 Bearcats arrived in 1949 to supplement the Hellcats and Bearcats and were operated by VF-711, VF-712, VF-713, VF-718 and

VMF-236.

VF-713 was called to active duty on 1 February 1951 and transitioned to F4U-4 Corsairs. The squadron was eventually augmented into the regular

Above, Denver-based F8F-2 sits on the ramp at Denver in the early 1950s. (via Menard)

Navy and was redesignated VF-152

At right, Denver reserve F8F-2 Bearcats passing over the Oakland Bay Bridge. (USN) Below, four Denver-based F8F-2s in flight in 1951. (E.M. Greenwood via Fred Roos)

on 24 January 1953.

Three serious Bearcat accidents occurred at Denver.The pilot of a VF-718 F8F-2, BuNo 121694, was killed when he flew into the ground during bad weather near NAS Denver on 17 March 1951. Another VF-718 pilot was killed during a forced landing at NAS Denver, CO, on 7 May 1951. The third incident took place on 28 July 1951 when a VMF-236 pilot exited the runway and ended up on his back. Luckily, the pilot survived because of the quick thinking of the ground crew. During its slide though the field, the cockpit filled with mud and the pilot quit breathing. Twenty or so sailors lifted the aircraft enough to clear the pilot's airway and revive him.

The Bearcats were replaced by F2H-1s and later F9F-6/7s.

Above, Denver-based F8F-2 BuNo 121619 in March 1952. Prop hub and drop tank tip were white. (Clay Jansson via Fred Roos) At right, Denver-based F8F-2 BuNo 121638 undergoes maintenance. (via Dave Menard)

After WWII, the Naval Air Reserve Training Unit was established at NAS Norfolk. The F8F-2 was flown between 1951-53 along with F4U Corsairs, FH-1s Phantoms, and F2Hs Banshees by VMF-223.

NAVAL AIR RESERVE NAS NORFOLK, VA

At right, ex-Norfolk-based F8F-2 BuNo 122674 after purchase for the civilian market. (B.R. Baker via Menard)

NAVAL AIR RESERVE NAS SPOKANE, WA

NAS Spokane was established as a Reserve Air Base on 1 September 1948 and disestablished on 1 February 1958.

NAS Spokane reserve F8F-2 Bearcat being armed with 20mm ammo on 16 July 1952. Spokane-based aircraft were identified with an "N" tail code. (National Archives)

NAVAL AIR RESERVE NAS SAINT LOUIS, MO

NAS St. Louis was operated as a Naval Air Reserve Base from 1946 through 1958. Starting out with F6F-5, -5E and -5P Hellcats, the fighter squadrons (VF-921, VF-922, and VF-923) added the FG-1D and F4U-4 Corsairs in 1946-47 before receiving Grumman F8F-1 Bearcats, FH-1 Phantoms and F2H-1 Banshees in 1951. St. Louis's Bearcats outlasted

the newer McDonnell Phantoms and Banshees, which were transferred out in 1952. The Bearcats and Corsairs eventually were replaced with Grumman F9F-4 Panthers in early 1954, which in turn were replaced by the swept-winged North American FJ-2 Fury in 1956-57.

Other aircraft flown at St. Louis were: SBW-4E/SB2C-4E Helldivers (1946-49), TBM-3E Avengers (1946-51), PV-2 Harpoons (1946-56), PBY-5A Catalinas (1946-50), AM-1 Maulers (1950-54, see Naval Fighters #24), AD-4NA Skyraiders (1954-56), TV-1/2 Shooting Stars (1954-57), P2V-5/5F Neptunes (1955-57), T-34B Mentors (1957), and a mixed bag of utility aircraft including the SNJ, SNB, JRB, R4D, and R5D.

Fighter squadrons VF-922, VF-923, and VMF-221 all utilized the

Bearcats as well as the other fighter types available at NAS St. Louis.

The only major Bearcat incident occurred when a pilot was injured during a forced landing after takeoff from NAS St. Louis, MO, in BuNo 95301 on 16 July 1951.

Even though the Navy left Lambert Field in 1958, the Air Force has continued to operate from St. Louis into the 21st century.

Below, thirteen Saint Louis-based F8F-1s with BuNo 95211 (U/14) third from left in 1951. (USN via Fred Roos)

Above, St. Louis-based F8F-1 BuNo 95017. (via Fred Roos) Below, St. Louis-based F8F-1 BuNo 95211 after a belly landing at Goodfellow AFB, TX, on 15 July 1953. (NMNA) Bottom, F8F-1 BuNo 95351 on 18 October 1950. (USN via Fred Roos)

NAVAL AIR RESERVE NAS GLENVIEW, IL

page 194).

Glenview-based F8Fs were involved in 5 accidents: BuNo 95004 was damaged when the gear collapsed during its landing roll-out at Glenview on 15 September 1950. A VF-722 F8F-1 BuNo 94833 was damaged in a collision on the runway at NAS Glenview on 18 February 1951. On 19 September 1951, F8F-2P BuNo 121659 ground-looped during a crosswind landing at NAS Glenview, IL, with minor damage to the aircraft. A second Bearcat, F8F-1 BuNo 94963, also ground-looped at Glenview on 19 September 1951. In bad weather, BuNo 95079 crashed into a mountain near Skull Valley, AZ,

In 1946, NAS Glenview became a Reserve Air Station and headquarters for the Naval Air Reserve Training Command. VF-722, VF-724, VF-726, and VMF-543 flew Bearcats at Glenview. The regular Navy set-up its CIC school at Glenview and utilized the Bearcat and other aircraft (see

on 15 November 1952 during a cross-country from Glenview to San Diego.

Above, Glenview-based VF-726 insignia. Below, four Glenview-based Bearcats in flight in 1950. (Clay Jansson)

Above, oil-soaked Glenview Reserve F8F-1 BuNo 94918 prepares to start its engine. (USMC via Fred Roos) Below, snowy NAS Glenview VF flightline in December 1950. BuNo 95233 is coded V/18. (Clay Jansson)

NAVAL AIR RESERVE
NAS GLENVIEW

Above, Glenview-based F8F-1 BuNo 94788 in July 1950. (Clay Jansson via Fred Roos) At right, Glenview-based F8F-1 BuNo 94827, also in July 1950. (Clay Jansson via Fred Roos) Bottom, Glenview-based F8F-1 BuNo 94951, also in July 1950. (Clay Jansson via Fred Roos)

The Blue Angels' origins can be traced to NAATC Jacksonville, FL, in 1946. The original team led by LCDR Roy M. "Butch" Voris was comprised of four instructors from the training command flying F6Fs in their spare time. The original intent was to show student pilots precision flying as it should be done. In a very short time, they were performing at Naval Air Stations and civilian air shows. They traded-in their Hellcats for F8F Bearcats in August and put on a spectacular performance at the 1946 Cleveland Air Races. They flew the nimble Bearcat until July 1949 when they picked-up the Grumman F9F-2 Panther. During July while working-up on the Panther, the unit continued putting on airshows in the Bearcats.

The last Hellcat airshow was at Grumman when the Blues picked-up their freshly painted and modified Bearcats. The team departed for Jacksonville the next day with the F8F-1s to commence the transition. Prior to departure, Butch quizzed the Grumman engineers about the need for compensating weight to balance out modifications, as was needed on the F6Fs. He was told it was not needed on the F8Fs. As Butch relates the story: "Our first stop was at Norfolk. As we approached and received landing instructions, we broke for single plane landings. On slowing and extending my landing gear, simultaneously back trimming for neutral stick force, the trim tab wheel reached the full nose-up metal-to-metal stop. I increased the back pull force on the stick to hold the nose up and called the tower to advise them that I had a control problem and was

pulling up and out of the landing pattern. This was followed by Wick, Al, and Billy doing the same. Not a second later, the tower frantically informed me that Grumman had grounded our aircraft as unsafe for flight. With some hasty experimentation, I found that I could slow to about 120 knots by holding the stick all the way against the back stop, and by using power to keep the nose from falling through. We landed at 40 knots above normal,

Below, Blue Angels in a stacked formation during a ferry flight. (USN via Fred Roos)

Above, the Navy's first adversary, the yellow "Beetle Bomb" BuNo 95187, flew as a simulated Japanese Zero during the Blue's demonstrations in 1948. (Chalmers Johnson via William Swisher) At right, this view of "Beetle Bomb" shows the underwing markings. (Fred Dickey via Dave Lucabaugh) Below, Blues #3 F8F-1 BuNo 94989 at the Oakland Airport in 1947. (W.T. Larkins via William Swisher)

with only slight longitudinal control remaining. We came very close to bailing out, or ditching in Norfolk harbor, a colorful ending for our just acquired Bearcats. It may well have spelled the end of the Blues."

Above, four Blue Angels' F8F-1s warm-up in preparation for an airshow at NAS Jacksonville in 1948. (K.D. Boyer via D. Lucabaugh) Below, Blue Angels #4 on the ramp before an airshow. Note US NAVY painted under the wing. (via Dave Menard)

1/48 SCALE HAWK/TESTORS F8F-2 BEARCAT

The Hawk 1/48 scale kit is the oldest Bearcat kit and was originally released in the 50s. It has been offered in numerous different boxes and was available at one time from Italeri. It is currently still available from Testors. It is a good kit for its age and includes bombs, rockets, open or closed cockpit and a pilot figure. The most often listed shortcoming of this kit is the shape of the engine cowl.

The oldest box top I have is dated 1967 and is for Kit #562, which is for a Quantico-based Bearcat. In addition, a chrome-plated version with Thai Air Force decals was offered at one time as was kit #589 with VF-61 (seen below) and "Beetle Bomb" markings. Testors kit #519 features a Glenview Reserve F8F-2 on the box top and optional decals for Major Al Williams' colorful Gulfhawk IV (see page 23-24).

1/200 SCALE X-MODEL F8F-1 & 1/144 SCALE CREATIONS CHAUBET F8F-1

The one-piece X-Models epoxy resin kit #X-6 has a wingspan of 2-1/8 inches. It has no propeller, no landing gear, and no decals.

The Creations Chaubet white metal F8F-1 kit #30 has eight pieces (aircraft, prop, main gear (2), gear doors (2), and tail wheel. Wing span is about 2-7/8 inches and like the X-Model kit it has no decals.

At right, size comparason between the 1/200 and 1/144 kits and the Monogram 1/72 F8F-1B. (models by Tom Healy)

MONOGRAM 1/72 SCALE F8F-1B BEARCAT

The Monogram 1/72 scale F8F-1B Bearcat kit was released in the late 60s and is an excellent offering in that scale. Like the Hawk kit, it has been offered in numerous different boxes. It included bombs, rockets, belly tank and open or closed canopy with a pilot figure and stand. The original box top (kit #PA144) 1967, 1973 (kit# 6789) and the 1989 re-release (kit #5013) depict a VF-20A F8F-1. The kit was released again in 1991 as kit #74006 with a French F8F-1B on the box top. The kit included optional decals for a Thai Air Force Bearcat.

1/72 SCALE SWORD BEARCAT KITS

Sword has produced two Bearcat kits. A US Navy one seen at right with decals for VF-3, VF-3A, VF-151 and a French Air Force version. The other Bearcat kit had markings for Vietnam and Thailand included. Any of the three fighter versions of the Bearcat can be made from these kits. Sword elected to include two fuselages to accomplish this goal. A short-tailed fuselage for the F8F-1 and F8F-1B and a tall-tailed fuselage so that an F8F-2 could be modeled. Both kits include resin detail parts including a cockpit tub, engine, gear well, rockets, and main gear tires and rims.

1/48 SCALE HOBBYCRAFT BEARCAT KITS

Hobbycraft released four Bearcat kits in 1996-97. They were: HC-1440 Blue Angels, HC-1441 French F8F-1B Indochina War, HC-1442 Vietnamese F8F-1, and HC-1443 US Navy F8F-2. These kits have optional parts to construct any one of the three fighter versions: the F8F-1, F8F-1B, and F8F-2. The kits included bombs, rockets, belly tank, and open or closed cockpit.

Bottom, Academy kit built by Lee Reinitz.